ASSEMBLIES
FOR ALL

Other titles

Lighting the Way: The case for ethical leadership in schools by Angela Browne

Riding the Waves: Finding joy and fulfilment in school leadership by James Hilton

Growth Mindset: A practical guide by Nikki Willis

Happy School 365: Action Jackson's guide to motivating learners by Action Jackson

The Wellbeing Toolkit: Sustaining, supporting and enabling school staff by Andrew Cowley

ASSEMBLIES FOR ALL

Diverse and exciting
assembly ideas for
all Key Stage 2 children

Paul Stanley

BLOOMSBURY EDUCATION

LONDON   OXFORD   NEW YORK   NEW DELHI   SYDNEY

BLOOMSBURY EDUCATION
Bloomsbury Publishing Plc
50 Bedford Square, London, WC1B 3DP, UK
29 Earlsfort Terrace, Dublin 2, Ireland

BLOOMSBURY, BLOOMSBURY EDUCATION and the Diana logo are trademarks of Bloomsbury Publishing Plc

First published in Great Britain, 2021 by Bloomsbury Publishing Plc

A catalogue record for this book is available from the British Library

ISBN: PB: 978-1-4729-7509-6; ePDF 978-1-4729-8884-3

2 4 6 8 10 9 7 5 3 (paperback)

Text design by Marcus Duck

Typeset by Newgen KnowledgeWorks Pvt.Ltd., Chennai, India
Printed and bound by CPI Group (UK) Ltd, Croydon CR0 4YY

Contents

Assemblies with accompanying slideshows

Acknowledgements

To Sue, Meg, Fred and Sid – I couldn't have done this without you all.

A big thank you to all the amazing colleagues and wonderful children I have worked with over the years, at Taverham Junior School, George White Junior School and West Earlham Middle School.

To Molly, a very good friend and colleague, whose creativity is inspiring.

Introduction

There is huge value in a whole school community gathering together at least once a week, to be exposed to, consider, discuss and explore a variety of significant themes and issues. It is vital that children understand topics such as humans' impact on the environment, racism, positive relationships, similarities and differences, diversity and bullying – and that they also celebrate achievement. I entered the teaching profession to further children's learning, knowledge and understanding, and their wonder and appreciation of the world around them: assemblies are the perfect vehicle for this.

None of the issues mentioned above, which all need to be addressed in a whole school context, are religious but schools do have a legal obligation to implement 'collective worship'. Although this is often ignored, most assembly resources currently available feature religious references and prayers as a result. I believe morality taught via a non-religious approach means all children are more likely to access the messages, so I have spent a number of years producing my own non-religious assemblies 'for all', the best of which are gathered in this book. This is not to say that I question the commitment to children's wellbeing and education of any religious organisation that I have worked with. For example, as headteacher of a Church of England school for ten years, I had a strong and positive relationship with members of the Christian community, but I do believe children should be free to choose their own religion, or not, and that school is not the place for 'collective worship'.

I am confident that these assemblies will provide interesting, inspiring, thought-provoking and worthwhile assemblies for primary school pupils, particularly those in Key Stage 2. The book is designed to be flexible, to be dipped into, and the assemblies have all been tried and tested over many years on real children – rather than those who exist in the imaginations of many of those who write assembly scripts! It is more important than ever that such themes and values are explored at a time when, sadly, the school curriculum is 'squeezed', narrow and results-driven. I hope the assemblies help to develop a moral framework without resorting to traditional religious teachings, and that you and the children enjoy, appreciate and learn from them.

Paul Stanley

Each assembly idea includes a 'script' for the assembly, as well as an overview of the assembly, its key message, a list of necessary resources and any set-up requirements. Assemblies 1 to 14 are standalone assemblies without accompanying slideshows. Assemblies 15 to 36 have accompanying slideshows, which can be accessed at www.bloomsbury.com. These assemblies can also be delivered without the accompanying slideshows, if needed. The assembly scripts indicate when to show each slide.

Assembly 1
My Favourite Things

Overview

An assembly that asks children to share what their favourite things are and consider what makes something truly 'valuable'.

Key message

The things we cherish most are those that have sentimental value. How much we value them rarely has anything to do with monetary worth.

Resources

- An object of sentimental value to you

Set-up requirements

Optional: display the text of the poem so children can follow it as you read.

Outline

1 Explain that you will be talking about your favourite things. Before you tell the children what these are, ask them what their favourite things are.

Answers are likely to be material things. If so, point out that there are many things more precious than material goods. If the children have mentioned favourite things such as photographs, loved ones or objects with sentimental value, this will link nicely with the next part of the assembly.

2 Show the children an object that is of sentimental value to you and explain why. (It could be a photo or photo album, a childhood possession, etc. It depends how much you want to 'give' of yourself.)

3 When we think about it carefully, the importance of an object pales into insignificance beside our ability to be alive, spend time with other people and appreciate the wonders of the world around us. Tell the children that this is your 'favourite thing'.

4 When we first thought about 'favourite things', the children may have thought of objects. However, many people with lots of 'things' and lots of money either don't appreciate them or those objects don't make them happy.

Some things which makes us truly happy are: friendships; family; feeling that we have done something well; or doing something we enjoy. The best things cost nothing at all but are priceless in sentimental value.

5 Finish by reading a poem which sums this up.

Treasure
by S Garratt

· ·

Hugs with my family, smiles from our neighbours,
Playing with friends, the kindness of strangers.
Cheering my team, singing a song,
Learning new things, and getting along
All of these things give me so much more pleasure
Than any amount of riches and treasure.

The wonders of nature: white clouds in blue sky,
The silvery moon, the heat of July,
A perfect pink rosebud, a blackbird's refrain,
The sweet scent of lilacs, refreshing cool rain,
Summer's bright sun and winter's ice-cold
Bring me more joy than silver and gold.

Colossal whales and slow-moving snails,
The freedom to roam through mountains and dales,
Watching the sun set over the sea,
Fields full of poppies, wind in the trees.
To me, a forest of oak, beech and ash
Is worth so much more than a pocket of cash.

My hands that help others, that carry and soothe,
My ears that hear poetry, music and truth,
My mouth that tastes mangoes and curry and cheese,
Ripe strawberries, caramel, fresh-podded peas.
My eyes that see beauty, colours and light
My legs that can run, jump and dance, day and night
The beat of my heart, laughter, good health
Have more value to me than money and wealth.

Assembly 2
Friendship

Overview

An assembly that looks at the importance of friendship and what being a good friend truly means.

Key message

Having good friends is wonderful and important, but it is not always easy. Being a good friend and overcoming any difficulties is something that we need to work at sometimes.

Resources

- A recording of *Nimrod* from the *Enigma Variations* by Edward Elgar, e.g. www.youtube.com/watch?v=d08YBZxMK_4
- A device to play the recording from
- Speakers
- Optional: a picture of Edward Elgar
- 10 sheets of A4 card

Set-up requirements

Play the recording of *Nimrod* as the children enter the assembly hall.

Optional: display the text of the poems so children can follow them as you read.

Outline

1 Tell the children that you're here today to talk to them about friendship.

Start by asking them:

- Does anyone recognise this piece of music?
- Can anybody name the title or composer?

Give the title of the piece and explain that it was written by a British composer called Edward Elgar. The whole piece of music is made up of 14 parts. Each part was written for a friend of Elgar's and is also about that friend – each part describes a different friend of Elgar's. The one they heard was about Elgar's best friend, Augustus Jaeger.

Reflect how lovely it would be to have a piece of music written for you and to have the talent to be able to celebrate your friends in this way.

2 Ask the children about friends.

- What makes a good friend?
- What does a good friend do?
- What qualities do they have?

As a child makes a suggestion, write the word or phrase on a piece of A4 card and ask the child to come up and hold it so that everyone can see it.

The children may mention qualities such as honesty, kindness, loyalty, helpfulness or trustworthiness. They may say a friend is someone who is always there for you; who is caring; who is someone you can talk to; or someone you can laugh with.

When enough suggestions have been made, read through each word. You may wish to explore the meaning of each word further.

Point out that it would be great if friends were like this all the time.

3 Explain that being a 'good friend' is sometimes quite a difficult thing. Ask the children to listen carefully to this poem about friendship. Friendship can be tricky at times, and this poem recognises that.

Best Friends
by Bernard Young

· ·

Would a best friend
Eat your last sweet
Talk behind your back
Have a party and not ask you?

Mine did.

Would a best friend
Borrow your bike without telling you
Deliberately forget your birthday
Avoid you wherever possible?

Mine did.

Would a best friend
Turn up on your bike
Give you a whole packet of your
favourite sweets
Look you in the eye?

Mine did.

Would your best friend say
Sorry I talked about you behind your back
Sorry I had a party and didn't invite you
Sorry I deliberately forgot your birthday
– I thought you'd fallen out with me

Mine did.

And would a best friend say
Never mind
That's OK.

I did.

Best Friends by Bernard Young, from 'What Are You Like?', Orange Socks Press.

This poem illustrates that sometimes we do and say things that, afterwards, we wish we hadn't. It's often this that makes us upset, angry or fall out, whether we are friends or not.

4 Read this short poem, which is about friendship and how to keep it going.

Always remember to forget
Anonymous

· ·

Always remember to forget
The things that made you sad
But never forget to remember
The things that made you glad.

Always remember to forget
The friends that proved untrue.
But don't forget to remember
Those that have stuck by you.

Always remember to forget
The troubles that have passed away.
But never forget to remember
The blessings that come each day.

5 Remind the children that the only way to have a friend is to be one. Let's try to be good friends, to our friends and to other people. Let's think of other people's feelings and remember that a kind word can make a big difference. Let's remember what makes a true friend.

Assembly 3
Being Thankful

Overview

An assembly that emphasises the importance of appreciating what we have, using a Polish folktale to present the message.

Resources

Seven masks, hats or signs for the children to wear as the characters: a farmer, two children, a wise woman, a chicken, a goat and a cow.

Key message

We should appreciate what we have and not be greedy. We should remember how lucky we are with what we already have.

Set-up requirements

You may wish to pre-select the children who will act out the story so they are prepared.

Outline

1 Choose seven volunteers to come to the front and give each child a mask, hat or sign to show which character they are playing. They will act out these parts while the following story is read aloud.

Explain that the story is an old Polish folktale.

2 Read the story, with the children acting their parts.

No room in the house
Polish folktale

Once upon a time, a farmer lived in a very small hut with his two children. They were happy but poor. Their hut was so small that there was no room for anything but a bed, a table and three small chairs.

As the children grew older, the farmer found it more and more difficult to live in such a tiny space, so he went to visit the wise woman in the village to see if she could help.

The wise woman thought long and hard about his problem. Finally, she asked: 'Do you have a chicken?'

'Of course I have a chicken,' said the farmer. 'I'm a farmer!'

'Then bring it to live in the house,' said the wise woman.

The farmer was very confused, but he returned home and brought the chicken to live inside the house with his family. But the chicken made life harder. It flapped and clucked and laid eggs everywhere.

The farmer went back to see the wise woman. 'I did what you advised. I took the chicken into the house, but it's even worse now. We have even less room than before. What shall I do?'

After a pause, the wise woman asked, 'Do you have a goat?'

'Of course I have a goat,' said the farmer. 'I'm a farmer!'

'Then bring it into the house,' she replied.

The farmer could not understand at all how that would help, but he was willing to give it a go, as he had no better ideas himself. So he went home and led the goat into the house. The goat was very happy about this: it particularly enjoyed nibbling the bedspread and jumping up on the table, but the farmer and his children weren't too pleased.

The very next day, he raced back to see the wise woman. 'Please help me,' he begged. 'My house is even more crowded now. What shall I do?'

'Aha!' said the wise woman. 'I suppose you have a cow?'

'Of course I have a cow,' said the farmer. 'I'm a farmer!'

'Then bring it into the house to live with you,' she replied.

Against his better judgement, the farmer did as the wise woman suggested. It came as no surprise to him that this did not help at all: the cow was massive, it knocked over all the chairs, and it was very smelly.

The children loved the animals, but even they were fed up with the cramped conditions and the smell. It was so noisy they couldn't sleep, so they begged their father to go back to the wise woman for some better advice, which he did.

'I have followed your advice,' said the farmer. 'But our home is worse than ever. We can barely move, and I don't know what to do.'

The wise woman was silent for a while, but finally she said, 'Go home, and take the cow and the goat back to the barn and the chicken back to its coop.'

Confused and bewildered, the farmer ran straight home and did exactly as he had been told. As he took the animals back to where they belonged, his children cleaned up the feathers, the eggs and the mess. The hut now looked quite homely again. There was room to breathe and move, and it was clean. The family realised that the hut was big enough after all. From that day on, they lived very happily together in their huge little hut.

3 Reinforce the message that sometimes we don't realise what we have until it is gone. The farmer didn't appreciate that his house was perfectly big enough for him and his family: he wasn't satisfied with what he had. It was only when the house became full of animals and was genuinely crowded that he realised how lucky he was.

Explain that sometimes we don't always realise how lucky we are, and we often take things for granted.

Remind the children that we should all remember to be grateful for the good things and experiences we have in our lives. We should also remember to express our gratitude to those around us. A thank you goes a long way.

Assembly 4
Peace

Overview

An assembly which discusses the meaning and importance of peace, as well as some symbols associated with it.

Key message

It is important that we all find peace and calm in our lives.

Resources

A bag which contains pictures of the following five things:

- an olive branch
- a CND sign
- a dove
- a rainbow
- Jelly Babies.

Optional: you may wish to have some packets of Jelly Babies to share with the children. Please check the children's dietary requirements if you do this.

Set-up requirements

None

Outline

1 Ask for six volunteers to come to the front of the assembly. Ask each child to remove one item from the bag. Give one of the children a handshake, instead of one of the five objects.

2 Ask the children in the audience if they can name each of the objects. Then ask them to guess what the connection between these objects might be.

3 Tell the children the answer: all these things symbolise peace. Explain the significance of each object and the handshake.

- An olive branch: an Ancient Greek goddess called Irene was often shown carrying an olive branch to symbolise peace. We still have the link between olive branches and peace today. The phrase 'extend an olive branch' refers to resolving arguments or conflicts and re-establishing peace. Tell the children to look closely next time they see an older British 50-pence piece – Britannia, the woman on the front, is holding out an olive branch.

- A CND sign: This symbol was invented in 1958 by the Campaign for Nuclear Disarmament, which campaigned to stop countries making nuclear bombs. It has been used as a peace symbol ever since.

- A dove: doves have been symbols of peace for thousands of years. In Ancient Greece, doves symbolised the renewal of life, while in Ancient Japan, a dove carrying a sword was the symbol for the end of conflict and war.

- A rainbow: rainbows have also been symbolic of peace for thousands of years, as they are like bridges that bring people together.

- Jelly Babies: Explain that 'Jelly Babies' were launched by the sweet-making company Bassett's in 1918 to celebrate the end of World War I. At the time, they were called 'Peace Babies' and quickly became popular. During World War II, production stopped because of a shortage of ingredients. They were 'reborn' in 1953 and renamed 'Jelly Babies'. Invite the children to consider why the sale of Jelly Babies was a good way to celebrate peace. Reflect that the Peace Babies marked a new beginning (babies). They showed that life was returning to normal and could be fun again.

- A handshake: This is an ancient symbol for peace, as shaking hands shows that there is no weapon in your hand or the hand of the person you are meeting.

4 Discuss the two meanings of peace: firstly, being free from war and conflicts; and secondly, a calm situation uninterrupted by noise, worries and so on.

5 Finish by emphasising the value of peace and quiet.

Explain that how important it is for us all to create moments of peace and quiet in our lives, so that we can reflect, think, unwind and enjoy some calm. We should value and appreciate peace and quiet, even if we have to switch off our electronic devices to achieve this!

Ask the children to close their eyes and be absolutely still and silent for a minute. Let them experience what this stillness and silence feels like.

Assembly 5
Creativity

Overview

An assembly that looks at the importance of creativity and encourages the children to think creatively.

Key message

Creativity is an important skill to have. It is useful to be able to interpret questions in different ways and see lots of different answers to a question.

Resources

- A large paper clip
- Six dictionaries
- A brick
- A flipchart and pen

Set-up requirements

None

Outline

1 Tell the children that this assembly is all about creativity. Ask the children what they think creativity is and what being creative means.

   Explain that creativity can be artistic, such as drawing, painting, photography or sculpture. It can also be physical, such as drama, dance or sport.

   But it can also involve thinking creatively. This is particularly important in problem-solving, inventing and in many jobs. People will always need skills like teamwork, problem-solving and creativity.

2 Show the children a large paper clip. Ask them how many uses they can think of for it. What ideas do they have? Congratulate the children who come up with the most creative ideas.

3 Hand out a dictionary each to six children. Ask them to open the books at a random page and choose an interesting word. (If they aren't happy doing this, tell them to pass the dictionary to their neighbour.)

   Write the first two words found on the flip chart. Ask if anyone can suggest an interesting sentence using both words.

   Ask if anyone else can add any extra creative ideas to the sentence.

   If you have time, repeat this with two different words.

4 Hold up a brick. Ask the children to think of different uses for the brick, the more creative the better. You could give some examples to start the children off, such as:

- to use as an ugly paper weight

- to pop bubble wrap quickly

- to mash potatoes

- to use as a goal post

- to demonstrate teamwork: one brick can't do anything – but many can make a house.

5 Ask the children how a person could be creative in a maths lesson, and discuss their suggestions.

6 Share some final thoughts.

Explain that creativity is the ability to interpret a question or situation in a different way and to be able to think of lots of different responses to it. Reiterate that this is a very useful skill and talent to have.

Explain that one creative idea can inspire another.

Remind the children that they should not be afraid to come up with imaginative ideas or responses to problems. There is rarely one answer to a problem.

Assembly 6
Humility

Overview

An assembly which discusses humility and pride.

Key message

Sometimes we need to ask for help and this is not a weakness. Humility is an important quality.

Resources

- A box of jumbled PE equipment (ropes, balls, bibs and so on)
- Eight A4 pieces of card with one letter from H, U, M, I, L, I, T and Y written on them

Set-up requirements

None

Outline

1 Show the children the box of jumbled PE equipment and ask for a volunteer to sort it out. Give them one minute to do so.

   After a minute, ask: What might help the volunteer to complete this task more quickly?

   Hopefully the children will come up with the answer: ask a friend to help. If not, suggest this option.

   Allow the volunteer to choose a friend to complete the task.

2 Explain that there are many situations when we should ask for help, but often we don't. Ask the children for suggestions why this might be. The children may mention that sometimes people feel that asking for help shows weakness or that it is embarrassing. They might also say that sometimes we believe we can do something on our own.

   Point out that it is important to ask for and accept help when we need it. No one should be too embarrassed or proud to ask for help, even though it's not always easy to admit we are struggling or not as good as we thought.

   Ask the children to imagine what could happen if we don't ask for help in the following situations:

   - Going somewhere new and getting lost
   - Starting a new school and not knowing the timetable or rules
   - Not understanding what to do in a lesson
   - Not knowing how a new toy or game works
   - Not knowing whether a meal contains an ingredient you are allergic to
   - Using a tool / machinery for the first time

  Assemblies for All © Paul Stanley, 2021

3 Explain that the quality we are thinking about is called humility. The word is an unusual and quite old-fashioned one. Ask for eight volunteers to come to the front. Give them the A4 letters and see if, between them, they can arrange them into a word that makes sense. Help them to spell it out if they struggle to find the answer.

Explore the meaning of humility.

- Not thinking you are always better than others and always know best. [You may want to point out that this is not the same as having a low opinion of yourself.]

- Not being worried about what others may think of you.

- Being unselfish.

- Being modest.

- Not being too proud, stubborn or arrogant to admit your mistakes and/or say sorry.

- Quietly getting on with being yourself.

- Doing things because it's the right thing to do.

Explain that 'humility' is not the same as being humiliated, when someone might make you feel silly on purpose – it is an entirely different word.

4 Ask the children to think for a moment about this very complex issue.

Reiterate that:

- Being proud of yourself is good.

- Being too proud can be a problem as it can prevent you asking for help.

- Being humble and showing humility can be a positive thing.

- When you are humble, other people are more likely to help you.

Assembly 7
Supporting Each Other

Overview

An assembly which illustrates that we all need other people's help at times.

Key message

We can all achieve so much more with the support of others.

Resources

- A video clip of the athlete Derek Redmond in the 1992 Olympics 400m final: https://vimeo.com/10926297
- A screen to play the video clip

Set-up requirements

Prepare the screen to play the clip.

Outline

1 Ask for four or five volunteers to come to the front of the assembly hall. Ask the volunteers to start running on the spot.

   After a while, ask them how long they think they could run for. Three minutes? How about three hours?

   Ask them how far they think they could run around the field or playground. Five times? Ten times?

   Thank the volunteers for their efforts and ask them to sit down.

2 Explain that there is a race that takes most people at least three hours to run. Ask if anyone knows what it is called (a marathon) and how far the race is (42.2 kilometres or 26.2 miles).

   Explain that some people take part in marathons to raise money for charity. They often run the race in heavy fancy dress costumes and their training takes many hours and a lot of dedication. Some people do the race by walking or in wheelchairs. Just like the best professional runners, they all need to keep going. They also need encouragement, because there will be times when they feel like giving up.

   The crowd at the side of the road at a marathon plays an important part in encouraging the marathon participants. In the same way, our friends and family can encourage us and help us reach our goals.

3 Different races require different skills and strength, but they all require dedication, stamina and perseverance.

   Explain that you are going to play a clip of the British athlete Derek Redmond, who was favourite to win the 400 m final in the 1992 Olympics. Ask the children to watch it and think about what we might learn from it.

(This short, powerful and moving clip shows Derek's sudden hamstring injury during the race. Despite this, after a short while, he continues the race in obvious great pain. Then a man appears on the track and puts his arm around Derek to help him reach the finish line, encouraged by cheering from the crowd. This man turns out to be his father.)

4 Reflect on what the video showed. Ask the children why they think Derek wanted to carry on to the end and didn't just give up. The children may mention his determination to finish, the support he had from his father or the encouragement he received from the crowd.

5 Finish by emphasising the following messages.

We can all achieve a lot more than we sometimes think, particularly if we have the love and support of others around us and a positive mental attitude to difficult situations and new challenges.

Likewise, it's important that we are always there to help, encourage and support our friends when they need us.

Assembly 8
Wisdom, Justice and
The Caucasian Chalk Circle

Overview

An assembly which explores the issues of justice, wisdom and parenthood through the story of Brecht's *The Caucasian Chalk Circle*.

Key message

Justice and wisdom involve seeing the whole picture clearly, and understanding what is important.

Resources

- A piece of chalk
- A doll
- Masks, hats or signs for the children to wear as the characters Azdak, Natella and Grusha

Set-up requirements

You may wish to pre-select the children who will act out the story so they are prepared.

Optional: display the text of the plot summary so children can follow it as you read.

Outline

1 Tell the children you are going to tell them the story of the play *The Caucasian Chalk Circle* by a German playwright called Bertold Brecht. The story is based on a play written in China hundreds of years ago, and different writers have written versions of the story since.

The Caucasian Chalk Circle: plot summary
Original play by Bertold Brecht

There was once a ruler called George. George and his wife Natella were very rich and had a baby son called Michael. However, it was a time of chaos in their land. One day, another leader took control and George's guards turned on him and killed him. Natella decided to flee for her life, taking as many riches with her as she could carry. But she left behind her son Michael. Luckily, Natella's servant, Grusha, rescued Michael.

Grusha was about to be married to a soldier called Simon, but she was so afraid for Michael's safety that she also fled the city. She took the baby to her brother's house in the countryside, where she hoped that Michael would be safe.

Unfortunately, soon after this, Grusha caught a fever and had to stay at her brother's house for a long time. While she was there, her brother convinced her to marry his friend Jussup, who was supposedly dying. After the wedding, Jussup admitted that he wasn't really ill – he was pretending to be ill so that he didn't have to fight in the war. Grusha was very angry that she had been tricked into a loveless marriage, but she could do nothing about it.

Years later, Simon the soldier bumped into Grusha. Grusha told him that her marriage was unhappy. Simon still loved Grusha, but assumed that Michael was Grusha's own child, so he left, broken-hearted.

Then some soldiers arrived in the village to take Michael back to his mother, Natella. Natella needed Michael back because without him, she couldn't gain control of her dead husband's lands and money.

Grusha pleaded with them not to take him, as she loved Michael like her own child, but they ignored her. She followed the soldiers and Michael back to the city, unsure what to do, but desperate to be near Michael and get him back.

The question of who should look after Michael would be decided in court by a judge. The judge was called Azdak.

So, Azdak was asked to decide who should look after Michael: his real mother Natella, or Grusha, who had cared for him. The first thing Azdak did was to draw a large chalk circle on the floor…

2 Draw a large chalk circle on the floor and put the doll in the centre of it. Ask for three volunteers to act out this part of the story as Azdak, Natella and Grusha. Then continue with the story.

Michael was put in the centre of the chalk circle. Azdak told Natella and Grusha to hold one hand each and to pull hard. Whoever could pull the child out of the circle would be the one to keep him. It was a tug-of-war situation, with Michael in the middle. Natella pulled him as hard as she could, but Grusha let go of his hand, unwilling to hurt Michael. Azdak ordered the women to do the same thing again, but once more, Grusha let go of Michael before he was hurt.

Azdak's decision was made.

'Only a true mother would risk her own happiness for that of her child,' he said. Grusha would be Michael's mother from now on.

Azdak also ordered that the lands and wealth should be given to Grusha. He granted Grusha an immediate divorce, allowing her to marry Simon.

3 Ask the children whether Azdak made the correct decision.

Discuss their views, and the following points:

• Who is the better mother, Natella or Grusha?

• Is being a good mother to do with birth? Riches? Power? Or love?

• How did watching the women and using a circle help Azdak make his decision?

4 Finish by reading the following nursery rhyme about wisdom.

A Wise Old Owl Sat in an Oak

A wise old owl sat in an oak

The more he saw the less he spoke

The less he spoke the more he heard.

Why aren't we all like that wise old bird?

Ask the children why the owl is wise, and discuss their answers.

5 End the assembly with some questions for the children to think about and take away.

- Was Azdak's decision wise?
- Is wisdom the same as common sense?
- Do you need to know a lot to be wise?
- Can anybody be wise?
- Do you have to be old to be wise?
- How do you become wise?

Assembly 9
Truth and Broken Promises

Overview

An assembly which illustrates that telling lies can have consequences, and that trust can take a while to build but can be quickly destroyed.

Key message

It is important to be able to trust one another. Others rely on us to keep our promises.

Resources

- Eight masks, hats or signs for the children to wear as the characters: a wolf, a boy, three sheep and three villagers

- Optional: a ring; a Cub, Brownie, Scout or Guide badge; a £10 note

Set-up requirements

You may wish to pre-select the children who will act out the story so they are prepared.

Outline

1 Explain that this assembly is about truth and lies. Ask for eight volunteers to play the wolf, boy, three sheep and three villagers.

2 Ask the children if they know the story of 'The Boy Who Cried Wolf'. Explain that the story is one of Aesop's fables. Aesop was a man who lived around 2,500 years ago and wrote many stories with important messages.

The volunteers act out the story as you tell it.

The Boy Who Cried Wolf
A retelling of one of Aesop's fables

Marco and his parents lived in a small village near some mountains. When he was ten years old, Marco's parents decided he was old enough to start looking after their flock of sheep. So that summer, Marco would lead the sheep up in to the mountains and stay with them while they grazed on grass, all day every day.

Unfortunately, Marco found sitting for hours on the grass very boring indeed, so one quiet sunny morning he decided to have some fun and pretend that something exciting was happening. At the top of his voice, he shouted, 'Wolf! Wolf! A wolf is chasing my sheep!'

Marco's parents and several other villagers came running up the mountain as fast as they could when they heard his shout. But when they arrived, all they could see were the sheep grazing quietly and Marco doubled up in laughter. The adults were angry with Marco for wasting their time, and he had a severe telling off from his parents for his prank. He felt ashamed and promised he wouldn't lie again.

Life went on as normal for a while, but after about a month Marco had forgotten his promise. He still found watching the sheep very tedious, so he decided it would be hilarious to play the same trick as before. He took the sheep up the mountain that morning as usual, but a short time later the villagers heard his yell.

'Wolf! Wolf! A wolf is chasing my sheep!'

Naturally the villagers ran to his aid, but, as before, there was no wolf to be seen.

Marco laughed and laughed when he saw the villagers' angry, red faces and thought it was the funniest joke ever. The villagers didn't agree. They were furious with Marco, and his parents sent him to bed straight after his tea. Marco promised he wouldn't lie again.

A few weeks passed by. Life carried on as normal, and Marco continued to graze his sheep on the mountainside each day. He still found it dull, but he whiled away the hours lying on the grass daydreaming. Then, one lazy sunny afternoon, he noticed the sheep acting nervously. They were bleating non-stop and darting about.

Marco knew something was wrong, but he couldn't believe his eyes when a huge wolf jumped out in front of him. Marco was speechless for a moment, but then started shouting: 'Wolf! Wolf! A wolf is chasing my sheep!'

Down in the village everyone heard his cries, but they all assumed Marco was playing yet another trick, so this time they completely ignored him. Nobody believed there really was a wolf and nobody ran up the hill to help.

At sunset, everyone started to wonder what had happened to Marco, and why he hadn't returned to the village with the sheep. His parents went up the mountain to find him. He was sitting on the ground weeping, surrounded by dead sheep.

'Why didn't you come when I raised the alarm? Why didn't you believe me?' Marco wailed.

'You lied to us before and that's why we didn't believe you,' one of the villagers explained.

Marco knew then that he would never tell a single lie ever again.

3 Ask the children what they think the message of the story is. Encourage them to discuss their thoughts about the story.

Emphasise the fact that the first two times Marco claims there is a wolf, the villagers are happy to trust him and are ready to help. But by the third time, Marco has lost people's trust, as he has lied and broken his promise.

4 Ask the children if they have ever made a promise? Or ever broken a promise?

5 Give some examples of promises and putting your trust in people.

- Wedding ring: when we get married, we promise we will love and care for each other for life.

- Club membership: for example, when you become a Cub, Brownie, Scout or Guide, you promise to do your best.

- £10 note: £10 notes say 'I promise to pay the bearer on demand the sum of ten pounds'. This is a promise that the note is worth £10, even though in reality it is simply a piece of paper or plastic.

Ask the children if they can think of further examples of promises or times when we place trust in others.

6 Reiterate the following messages to the children:

- We sometimes get it wrong and break promises. Occasionally we might make silly promises we can never keep. But most of us, most of the time, must make and trust promises in order for our society to work successfully.

- It takes a long time to build up trust, but that trust can be lost very quickly if you lie or break promises. You have to work very hard to rebuild trust once it's lost. If you have a reputation for lying, people won't trust you even when you're telling the truth.

We need to show others that we can be trusted to keep our promises and can be relied upon. Promises are important and we need to make them carefully. We need to respect other people's promises too.

Assembly 10
Respect for All Living Things

Overview

An assembly which asks children to consider whether some animals are more important than others.

Resources

Pictures of the following animals: snake, spider, fox, rabbit, tiger, ant, bee, swan, fly, moth, earthworm, crab, trout and dodo.

Key message

We should respect every creature because they are all important. All living things are connected and dependent on each other.

Set-up requirements

Optional: display the text of the poem so children can follow it as you read.

Outline

1 Ask the children if anyone has a favourite animal. Ask why they like that particular animal.

2 Ask for 14 volunteers to come to the front. Ask each child to hold up one animal picture.

Ask all the children which animals they would choose if we could only save six of these animals. Ask for hands up for a vote on this and organise the volunteers into two groups: survive and don't survive.

It is likely that the children will choose the more 'cute' and often more appreciated animals, such as rabbits or tigers, over insects such as flies or moths.

3 Explain that although some of these animals may seem more appealing to the children, every animal has a value. Without some animals, many other animals, including humans, wouldn't survive. Different animals (and plants) that live in the same area are all linked in some way: this is called an ecosystem. Often, the least appealing animals are especially useful to the ecosystem.

Expand on this by giving the children the following facts about some of the animals:

· Spiders eat insects. This means they prevent insect populations from getting too large, so the environment is not overrun with insects.

· Snakes' venom (poison) saves lives. Medicines developed from snakes' venom can be used to treat many serious illnesses, such as strokes, heart disease or Parkinson's disease.

· Ants help create healthy soil and help spread seeds so plants can grow and spread.

· Earthworms also help improve the quality of soil so plants are able to grow better.

· Horseshoe crabs' blood is used to check many medical things, such as vaccines, medicines and medical devices such as pacemakers, to ensure they are free of dangerous bacteria.

- Moths can give us vital clues to changes in our own environment, such as the effects of new farming practices, pesticides, air pollution and climate change.

- Bees pollinate many vegetables and fruit, such as beans, tomatoes, onions, carrots, broccoli, cantaloupes, pumpkins, watermelons and apples. Without bees, we wouldn't have these foods.

4 Ask if anyone has heard of the bird called a dodo. Explain that there are no longer any dodos on the planet: the species is extinct. Their extinction was because of humans.

The story of the dodo

The dodo used to live on the island of Mauritius, off the coast of eastern Africa. The dodo was about one metre tall, with a large beak and very small wings. It could no longer fly because it didn't need to fly as it had no predators – none of the other animals on Mauritius ate it.

In the 1500s, ships started stopping at the island. The sailors on the ships found that dodos were good to eat, so many dodos were hunted and killed.

Pigs and monkeys were brought to the island. Many ships had rats on board, and they escaped onto the island. These animals ate the dodos' eggs, so fewer dodos were born.

Within 100 years of humans being on Mauritius, the dodo had become very rare. By 1681, the last dodo had been killed. The dodo was extinct. Sadly, it wasn't only the dodo that became extinct: 23 other bird species also died out.

5 Share some facts about extinction.

- In the past 500 years, at least 1,000 animal and plant species have become extinct. Before this, thousands of species had already disappeared.

- Nobody knows how many species are currently in danger of becoming extinct because scientists don't know how many species exist, but dozens of species are becoming extinct every day.

- Extinction can be a natural process if an animal is not suited to the habitat it lives in. But around 99% of currently threatened species are at risk because of human activities.

Continues over the page

6 Read this extract. Ask the children to reflect on what they have heard while listening to it.

Hurt No Living Thing
Christina Rossetti

· ·

Hurt no living thing:

Ladybird, nor butterfly,

Nor moth with dusty wing,

Nor cricket chirping cheerily,

Nor grasshopper so light of leap,

Nor dancing gnat, nor beetle fat,

Nor harmless worms that creep.

7 Ask the children whether we should show the same respect to all animals, or whether some animals have more right to respect than others. Encourage them to explain their thoughts.

All living creatures are equally important. We all depend on each other for survival.

Assembly 11
Compassion for Farm Animals

Overview

An assembly which considers the concept of compassion and the issue of intensive farming.

Key message

Compassion is important; we should extend our compassion to farm animals.

Resources

- Two desks
- Eight chairs
- A bucket
- Marker cones
- A large fake medicine bottle (could be a glass bottle with a label saying 'Medicine')
- Optional: the documentary *Animals and Us* produced by Compassion in World Farming: www.ciwf.org.uk/education/films/farm-animals-us

Set-up requirements

Mark out a space at the front of the assembly using the cones. Put the two desks and four of the chairs there.

Optional: prepare the screen and speakers so you can play the video clip.

Outline

1 Tell the children that today you are talking about a concept called compassion. Compassion is feeling sympathy or pity for someone who is in a difficult situation. Today we are focusing on how we can show compassion towards animals, in particular farm animals.

2 Ask the children to name some farm animals. Can they explain which foods are produced from each animal they name?

Point out that meat, eggs and milk are commonly eaten foods. Explain that this means there is a lot of pressure for farmers to produce meat, eggs and milk as cheaply as possible so that they and the supermarkets can make more money. There is also a pressure to produce as much meat, eggs and milk as possible. This leads to animals being farmed in a way which is known as intensive farming.

But what does intensive farming mean? Explain that you will demonstrate by showing how it would work in a school.

3 Ask four children to volunteer to demonstrate the concept of 'intensive schooling'.

- Explain that the marked-out space with two desks and four chairs represents a classroom. Ask the four volunteers to sit at the desks.

- Suggest that if we get rid of the desks, we can fit more children in the 'classroom'. Remove the desks, add the four extra chairs, and ask for four more volunteers to come and sit down.

- Suggest that if we get rid of the chairs, we can fit even more children in the 'classroom'. Remove all the chairs, and ask for more volunteers.

- Suggest that if we get rid of the playground, we can build more classrooms and fit more children in the school.

- Suggest that if we get rid of the toilets, we will save space, time and money cleaning – but we will need a bucket: place this in the 'classroom'.

- Suggest that if we get rid of the kitchen and dining hall, we can save even more money as we can feed the children in the classroom. Food is very expensive so maybe we could just have drinks with lots of medicine in, to prevent any diseases being caused by being in such a small space.

Ask the children:

- Would they want to be at a school that was organised like this?

- Would it be fair or right to have a school organised in this way?

- So, is it OK for animals to live on farms which are organised like this?

4 If you feel it is appropriate, show the first five minutes of the documentary *Animals and Us* produced by Compassion in World Farming. The video shows that farm animals are more intelligent than we might think.

5 After watching the film (or without watching the film), ask the following questions:

- Should we show compassion to animals? How? Why?

- Should we treat farm animals differently to pets?

- Should we be thinking about where our meat, eggs and milk come from?

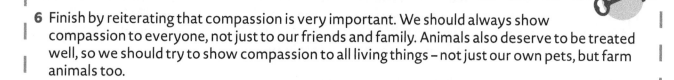

6 Finish by reiterating that compassion is very important. We should always show compassion to everyone, not just to our friends and family. Animals also deserve to be treated well, so we should try to show compassion to all living things – not just our own pets, but farm animals too.

Assembly 12
New Year's Resolutions

Overview

An assembly which initially explores some New Year traditions, and then explains how New Year's Resolutions can help us improve our lives.

Key message

New Year is often seen as a fresh start, so it is a time to make resolutions to improve something in our lives.

Resources

- A slice of bread
- A piece of coal
- Some coins
- A piece of ivy or other greenery

(You could use photos of these things instead, if you prefer.)

Set-up requirements

Optional: display the text of the poem so children can follow it as you read.

Outline

1 Explain that you will be talking about activities which are traditionally done at New Year. Remind the children that different countries across the world celebrate New Year at different times, but you will be focusing on British traditions.

Ask four children to come and hold up props.

Explain that one tradition is called 'first footing'. In Scottish and northern English folklore, the first person to enter a home on New Year's Day is said to bring good fortune for the coming year. It is said that it is luckiest if this person is a tall, dark stranger. He should appear at midnight on 1 January and give different things to the people in the house, as follows:

- bread, to ensure all have enough food for the next year
- coal, to ensure the house is always warm (ask if any of the children knows what coal is)
- money, to ensure prosperity over the next year
- greenery, to ensure all have a long life.

This visitor would then traditionally take away some ash, to signify the end of the old year.

2 Mention another unusual tradition. In medieval times – around 700 years ago – a flat cake would be put on the horns of a cow. The farmworkers would sing a song and dance around the cow until the cake fell to the ground. If the cake landed in front of the cow this meant good luck, but if it fell behind the cow it was bad luck.

3 One important and long-lasting tradition is to make a New Year's resolution. Ask the children if they know what a New Year's resolution is.

Explain that New Year can be a time for a fresh start as people look forward to the year ahead. Many people therefore see it as a time to change things and make themselves better people.

Ask if any of the children can think of resolutions their parents have made. Point out that many adults' resolutions involve giving things up, such as chocolate, smoking or alcohol. Suggest that resolutions can be positive as well, such as resolving to do more exercise or learn a new language.

Ask whether any of the children have had resolutions suggested to them by their parents. Children may come up with examples such as 'stop biting your fingernails' or 'keep your room tidy'. Remind them that their resolutions can be positive, such as trying to smile more often, to get on better with others or to help out more at home.

Stress that we often need the support of friends and family, so it can be a good idea to tell them your 'promise' or resolution and ask them to help you keep it.

Explain that you know that this is a good school, but if you had to think of a New Year resolution for the whole school, what would it be?

4 Explain that a new year is like an adventure into the unknown, like climbing a hill and not knowing what's on the other side, or walking along a road not knowing what's around the corner. There are lots of things we don't know about or can't control, but we can control our own behaviour and how we treat other people. This can make a big difference to whether we have a happy year or not.

5 Finish with a short poem, which emphasises the importance of taking time to enjoy life and do things. Ask the children to listen carefully and think about how they could use this message to make a positive difference to their own lives.

Take Time
Author Unknown

· ·

Take time to work, it is the price of success.

Take time to think, it is the source of power.

Take time to play, it is the secret of perpetual youth.

Take time to read, it is the foundation of wisdom.

Take time to be friendly, it is the road to happiness.

Take time to dream, it is hitching your wagon to a star.

Take time to look around, it is too short a day to be selfish.

Take time to laugh, it is the music of the soul.

Take time to love and be loved.

Assembly 13
Responsibility

Overview

An assembly that promotes taking responsibility and encourages being proactive and helpful.

Key message

We all need to take responsibility at times. We can't expect others to do things for us all the time.

Resources

- Four A4 pieces of card with the following words written on them: Everybody, Somebody, Anybody and Nobody
- A chair

Set-up requirements

Place the chair at the front of the assembly room.

Optional: display the text of the poem so children can follow it as you read.

Outline

1 Ask for four volunteers to come to the front. Give them one of the A4 cards each.

2 Read the following story and ask the children to hold up their card when their 'name' is mentioned.

> This is a story about four people named Everybody, Somebody, Anybody and Nobody. There was an important job to be done and Everybody was sure that Somebody would do it. Anybody could have done it, but Nobody did it. Somebody got angry about that, because it was Everybody's job. Everybody thought Anybody could do it, but Nobody realised that Everybody wouldn't do it. It ended up that Everybody blamed Somebody when Nobody did what Anybody could have done.

3 Ask the child playing Nobody to stand well to one side and put their Nobody sign on the empty chair.

Re-read the story to help the children make sense of it. As Nobody is no longer represented by a person, it reinforces the message of the story.

Then ask the children:

- Who should have done the job?

- What does this story tell you?

4 Read the following poem about 'Mr Nobody'.

Mr Nobody

Author Unknown

I know a funny little man,
As quiet as a mouse,
Who does the mischief that is done
In everybody's house!
There's no one ever sees his face,
And yet we all agree
That every plate we break was cracked
By Mr. Nobody.

'Tis he who always tears out books,
Who leaves the door ajar,
He pulls the buttons from our shirts,
And scatters pins afar;
That squeaking door will always squeak,
For prithee, don't you see,
We leave the oiling to be done
By Mr. Nobody.

He puts damp wood upon the fire
That kettles cannot boil;
His are the feet that bring in mud,
And all the carpets soil.
The papers always are mislaid;
Who had them last, but he?
There's no one tosses them about
But Mr. Nobody.

The finger marks upon the door
By none of us are made;
We never leave the blinds unclosed,
To let the curtains fade.
The ink we never spill; the boots
That lying round you see
Are not our boots, – they all belong
To Mr. Nobody.

Ask the children what the message of the poem is.

5 Finish by explaining that we shouldn't assume somebody else will do a job or clear up our mess for us: we should be doing it ourselves, and helping each other. Explain that it is important for all of us to take some responsibility at times and for all of us to help each other. It makes tasks much easier if we do.

Assembly 14
Service to Others

Overview

An assembly which explores the concept of volunteering.

Key message

We should appreciate those who give their time to help others. We should consider if we can do this too.

Resources

- 12 A3 cards, ready printed with the motivations (see below)
- Pictures of people whose jobs are to help others, such as: police officers, care home workers, medical staff, mountain rescue, firefighters, customer service staff, teachers or rubbish collectors
- A screen to display the pictures

Set-up requirements

Set up the screen to show the pictures.

Outline

1 Ask the children what they think the word 'service' means. Discuss their ideas and then explain that service is 'the action of helping or doing work for someone'.

2 Show the pictures and explain that the people in the pictures are paid to help others. Many of them choose these jobs because they want to and enjoy helping other people.

3 Explain that there are people across the country who help in all sorts of ways and don't get paid at all. They are called volunteers.

   - 11.9 million people did voluntary work at least once a month in 2018–19. Around 19.4 million did some voluntary work during that year.

   - Ask the children whether they know anyone who volunteers, and what they do – hands up. The children may need prompting to recognise people they know as volunteers, e.g. leaders for clubs such as football teams or Brownies. Ask the children for a show of hands if they go to Cubs, Brownies, Scouts or Guides, or belong to a football club or sports club, where adults help them.

4 Ask the children to share their ideas about why anyone would work for nothing. Then ask for 12 children to come to the front and hold up the prepared cards that show these different motivations for volunteering:

   - Give something back to an organisation that has helped you or your family

   - Make a difference to the lives of others

   - Help the environment

- Help others who are less fortunate or without a voice

- Feel valued and part of a team

- Spend quality time away from work or a busy lifestyle

- Gain confidence and feel good about yourself

- Gain new skills, knowledge and experience

- Improve your chance of getting a job

- Use your professional skills and knowledge to benefit others

- Meet new people and make new friends

- Get to know the local community

5 Explain that it may seem as if volunteering is just something for older people, but we can still be 'of service' to each other in school. Ask the children for suggestions of how we could do this.

   Some examples might be:

- Tidy up litter

- Hand in lost property

- Tidy up equipment

- Tidy the classroom

- Don't make a mess in the toilets

- Play with other children who might need a friend

- Tell staff if there is a problem

- Offer to take on roles such as register monitor or captain of a sports team

Reiterate that we all have a part to play in making our community and our school a happier and more positive place.

6 Remind the children of the importance of volunteers in their own lives. We should all appreciate the people who give their time and energy to help others. They have skills and expertise which can benefit us and they help because they want to, not because they are paid to.

Finish by asking the children to make a point of saying thank you to any volunteers they know next time they see them. It is great to show them that you appreciate their hard work.

Assembly 15
A New Start

Overview

An assembly which talks about new starts and emphasises the importance of being welcoming to each other.

Key message

New starts can be both exciting and daunting but we should try to embrace new opportunities. It's also important to make people feel welcome.

Resources

- Seven A4 pieces of card with one letter from W, E, L, C, O, M and E written on them
- Slideshow 1
- A screen to display the slideshow

Set-up requirements

Set up the screen to display the slideshow.

Outline

1 Welcome the children back to school after the summer holiday. Welcome your new pupils and new (or returning) teachers.

2 *Show slide 2.* Discuss with the children how each picture represents a new start. Point out that a new school year also represents new opportunities and a new start.

3 Say that you want to start by talking about a word that is particularly important at this time of the school year.

Invite seven volunteers to stand at the front of the assembly. Hand each child an A4 card with their letter and ask them to show their letters to everyone.

Ask the volunteers to work out what the letters spell and to rearrange themselves in the right order to make the word 'welcome'.

Ask the children why this is an important word for this time of the year. Answers may include: some people are new to the school and might feel nervous; it's important that everyone in our school feels comfortable and part of our school community; everybody likes to feel welcome as it makes us feel warm, settled, happy, comfortable and wanted.

4 Ask the children for ideas of how they can be welcoming to each other in school. These may include:

- Smiling, eye contact and positive body language, such as waving
- Thanking people when they help you
- Asking how people are and whether they need any help
- Making people who are new feel at home by introducing yourself to them and asking them to play

5 Talk about the excitement of new experiences. The new school year is exciting, but some people might feel a bit nervous too. Say that you hope the children are all excited about and looking forward to new experiences and challenges.

Emphasise that we are never too old to have new experiences and learn new things – even the teachers in school are learning all the time. Give an example of something you have recently experienced for the first time.

Now ask the children to give examples of any new experiences they had over the summer holiday.

6 *Show slide 3*. Read the questions, pausing between each one, and ask the children to think quietly to themselves about their own answers.

· What are you looking forward to this year?

· What are you nervous about?

· What new chance or experience would you like to have?

· What would you like to do better than last year?

· How would you like to be different from last year?

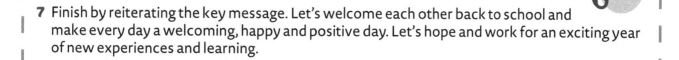

7 Finish by reiterating the key message. Let's welcome each other back to school and make every day a welcoming, happy and positive day. Let's hope and work for an exciting year of new experiences and learning.

Assembly 16
Paper and Perseverance

Overview

An assembly that considers and demonstrates the importance and value of perseverance, and how it can inspire others.

Key message

Even when we are in difficult situations, perseverance, hope and determination can help us and inspire others.

Resources

- A large piece of paper
- An origami paper crane, prepared earlier but hidden from view. Instructions are available here: www.activityvillage.co.uk/sites/default/files/downloads/origami_crane_instructions.pdf
- Slideshow 2
- A screen to display the slideshow

Set-up requirements

Set up the screen to display the slideshow.

Outline

1 Ask if anyone knows what origami is. Explain that origami is the Japanese art of paper folding, and that you are going to show them how to make a type of bird called a crane from paper. Show the crane picture on *slide 2*.

2 Start to make a paper crane. While you do so, explain that in Japan the crane is considered a very important creature. It symbolises good fortune because it was believed to live for one thousand years.

3 Halfway through, when it seems to be taking too long, pretend to get frustrated.

'Oh, this isn't working, I think I'll give up!'

Ask the children: 'Shall I give up, or carry on?'

4 Explain that, however tempting it may sometimes be to give up, it is much more worthwhile and satisfying in the long run to carry on and succeed in doing something.

Produce an origami paper crane that you made earlier. Explain that although you found it very difficult and time-consuming, you kept persevering because you wanted to show it to the children to illustrate the following story.

5 Tell the children that you want to tell them about a girl called Sadako Sasaki who lived in a Japanese city called Hiroshima in the last century.

Show the picture of Sadako Sasaki on *slide 3*.

Show the picture of Hiroshima on *slide 4*. Explain that in 1945, during World War II, an atomic bomb was dropped on Hiroshima, and nearly the whole city was destroyed in seconds.

Although many people were killed immediately, Sadako, who was only two at the time, survived. Many of those who survived developed leukaemia (a type of cancer) a few years later. This was caused by the radiation from the bomb. Sadly, this was the case for Sadako, who became ill in 1955.

While Sadako was in hospital, she heard about a Japanese legend which promised that anyone who folded a thousand origami cranes would be granted a wish by a crane. Sadako was really keen to do this, so she learned how to fold cranes in her hospital bed, using paper from anywhere she could find it – such as scraps, wrapping paper and medicine packets.

Very sadly, Sadako's condition became worse and she died at the age of 12, by which time she had reached her goal of folding over one thousand cranes, through her determination and perseverance. After her death, Sadako's friends and schoolmates raised funds to build a memorial to her and all the children who had died from the effects of the atomic bomb.

Show slide 5. In 1958, a statue of Sadako holding a golden crane was unveiled in the Hiroshima Peace Memorial Park. She became internationally recognised as a symbol of the innocent victims of war.

6 Ask the children to pause for a moment to think about Sadako and how she inspired others with her hope, her perseverance and her determination to make one thousand cranes, even though she was very ill.

Ask the children to think about the horrors of war and particularly about all the children who have been killed during or because of wars, and are sadly still living and dying in countries torn apart by war.

7 Finish by encouraging the children to make a paper crane themselves in their own time, if they would like to do so.

Remind them that it is important to carry on, no matter how difficult it is to do so.

Assembly 17
Justice and Fairness

Overview

An assembly which introduces the concept and tradition of justice, and helps children appreciate that there might be a difference between justice and fairness.

Key message

Life does not always seem fair, but justice and fairness are important. Finding just and fair solutions to problems requires wisdom and careful consideration.

Resources

- A chair
- A purse (placed under the chair)
- A cap for the child playing Gregory
- A tie for the child playing Edgar
- A crown for the child playing Queen Verity
- Slideshow 3
- A screen to display the slideshow

Set-up requirements

Set up the screen to display the slideshow. You may wish to pre-select the children who will act out the story so they are prepared.

Outline

1 Explain that today we are discussing the theme of justice. Ask the children if they can define this word.

2 *Show slide 2.* Explain the definition of each word.

- Justice: people being treated fairly and reasonably. Justice is an action that is morally right and fair.

- Fairness: treating people in an impartial, unbiased way – without showing favouritism or discriminating against anyone. Fairness aims for equal treatment for everyone.

3 *Show slide 3.* Explain that not getting your own way is not the same thing as something being unfair.

4 *Show slide 4.* Explain that there are symbols of justice, such as Lady Justice.

Explain that the history of Lady Justice goes back thousands of years to Roman times. Justice was one of the virtues celebrated by the Roman emperors.

Lady Justice is a symbol of fair and equal justice around the world. There is a statue of Lady Justice at Central Criminal Court of England and Wales in London.

Lady Justice is usually depicted with scales, a blindfold and a sword. Ask the children what each symbol might represent.

- Scales: The scales represent the weighing of evidence or weighing up right and wrong.

- Blindfold: The blindfold represents impartiality, which is the idea that justice should be applied to everyone equally, however rich or powerful and whatever their background.

- Sword: The sword represents the idea that justice can be swift and final.

5 Ask for three volunteers to come to the front of the assembly to act out the following story while you tell it.

Queen Verity's Justice
Folktale

Rumours were flying around the town. A rich merchant called Edgar had lost a purse full of gold coins and the person who found it had been promised a handsome reward. All the townspeople were rushing around searching every building, every alleyway, every corner, desperate to find the gold.

A stranger happened to be passing through the town that day. His name was Gregory and he was a poor pedlar who walked from town to town, village to village, selling brushes and brooms.

He had worked up an appetite on his travels, so he found a pub where he ordered a hearty bowl of soup, and sat down at a bench to eat. As he sat down, he felt something soft under his feet so he picked it up. It was a crimson velvet purse stuffed full of gold coins.

Gregory's heart raced with excitement, as he had heard the rumours like everyone else in town. He asked the innkeeper where he could find the merchant Edgar so that he could return the purse to him and claim his reward, and then he hurried off to find Edgar.

Edgar was delighted to see his money again, but he was not an honest man. He realised he could play a trick to avoid paying Gregory his reward.

Edgar opened the purse and shouted: 'Where are the rubies that were in the bag along with the gold coins? Gregory, you have stolen them!'

Gregory was taken aback by this false accusation. 'There were no rubies, sir. I have stolen nothing.'

'Give me back my rubies, you scoundrel, or you will have no reward at all,' responded Edgar.

Gregory was outraged. 'I am no thief, sir. Please come with me to see the queen: she is a wise woman and I am sure she will listen to us and treat us fairly.'

So Edgar and Gregory managed, not without some difficulty, to secure an appointment to meet with Queen Verity.

The queen listened to the story with great interest and watched the two men carefully. After a thoughtful pause, she asked Edgar: 'Do you swear that the bag you lost contained both gold coins and rubies?'

'I swear,' said Edgar.

'And do you, Gregory, swear that the bag you found had no rubies in it?'

'Yes,' said Gregory.

'Then there is your answer,' pronounced the queen. 'This can't be Edgar's velvet purse as there are no rubies in it. So it must belong to someone else. If no one claims it in a month, then the purse and the money will be yours to keep, Gregory.'

Edgar's mouth dropped open at this verdict. He could not believe what he had heard. He had lost his money.

'Maybe someone will find your bag too, Edgar,' said Queen Verity, with a wink.

6 Finish by showing the questions on *slide 5*. Ask for a show of hands for the first three questions.

Explain that questions 4 and 5 are for the children to take away to think about for themselves.

- Was what Queen Verity decided 'unbiased and reasonable'?
- Was Queen Verity's decision fair?
- Did she do the right thing?
- Is justice the same as being fair?
- Is life always just and fair?

Assemblies for All © Paul Stanley, 2021

Assembly 18
Overcoming Adversity

Overview

An assembly which looks at the life of Christopher Reeve, and explains that it is possible to overcome adversity if we have the right attitude and support.

Key message

We can deal with difficult situations if we remain positive.

Resources

- A pair of glasses
- A pair of red pants
- A jar of 'Kryptonite'
- Slideshow 4
- A screen to display the slideshow

Set-up requirements

Set up the screen to display the slideshow.

Outline

1 Ask the children to raise their hands if they would like to be a superhero.

Ask the children what they would want their superpowers to be. You could offer them a few suggestions, such as the ability to fly or to be invisible.

Ask three volunteers to come to the front to hold up the three props: glasses, pants and 'Kryptonite'. Ask the children who these things might belong to.

2 *Show slide 2.* Explain that today we are talking about a particular superhero. Give a brief biography of Christopher Reeve:

- Christopher Reeve played Superman in a series of films in the 1980s.

- In 1995 he played a policeman paralysed by injury in the film *Above Suspicion*. At the time, he spoke about the horror of losing everything we take for granted.

- A week after the film was released in cinemas, he fell off his horse, broke his neck and was paralysed. The man who had played Superman could no longer walk.

- Despite his severe injury, he carried on directing and acting in films and wrote books.

- He set up a charity to raise money and awareness about spinal injury.

- He died in 2004 after years of living and working with his disability.

3 *Show slide 3.*

Explain that people were amazed by how positive Christopher Reeve was despite what had happened to him. He said he could appreciate what he was able to do, rather than what he had lost. 'I am a very lucky guy. I can testify before Congress. I can raise funds. I can raise awareness.'

Christopher Reeve also said, 'Once you choose hope, anything is possible.'

4 Ask the children to sit quietly for a moment and think of all the things that we take for granted. These will depend on their experiences but may include things such as health, food, shelter, freedom and clean water.

Point out that Christopher Reeve also said that we should all be very grateful for what we have, and that we should try and make more effort to show our appreciation. He said: 'Gratitude, like love, needs to be active.' This means that it is not enough to just be grateful, we need to show it and say it.

Ask the children to think also of the people we take for granted: our parents and carers and families, our teachers and school staff. Do we show these people that we appreciate what they do for us?

5 *Show slide 4.*

Remind the children that Christopher Reeve achieved many things despite his disability. Ask the following questions:

- What is a superhero? Someone with special powers, or someone who can overcome difficulties?

- Was he a superhero just in his films, or did he prove to be more of a superhero in real life?

Assembly 19
Truthfulness

Overview

To explore and consider different shades of truth and to understand why being truthful is important.

Resources

- Slideshow 5
- A screen to display the slideshow

Key message

Telling the truth is important, but there are usually ways to tell the truth without hurting other people's feelings.

Set-up requirements

Set up the screen to display the slideshow.

Outline

1 Start with a quick game. Read the three possible definitions of each of the following words on the three slides and ask the children to choose which they think is the correct definition.

(The answers are: A, B and C.)

Show slide 2.

Tachydidaxy

  A An extremely fast type of teaching

  B A type of South American anteater

  C A black rock found only in Finland

Show slide 3.

Zamboorak

  A A type of xylophone, with the note bars made of coconut shells

  B A small cannon, mounted and fired from the back of a camel

  C A tropical fruit with red flesh

Show slide 4.

Sniggle

  A To run on tiptoes

  B A wooden tool used in weaving

  C To fish for eels by throwing bait into their hiding place

2 *Show slide 5.* Ask the following questions:

- Was I lying when I made up some of the definitions?

- Do you always believe what your teachers say?

3 Ask the children to consider that stories in books are made up.

- Is a story a 'lie'?

- If someone is telling or writing a story, are they telling the truth?

4 *Show slide 6.* Invite the children to consider the following situations. Give them time to think about each scenario:

- Someone you know is in hospital and you are visiting them. You think they look quite ill.

  – This is the truth, but do you tell them this? Or would that be unkind and make the person feel worse?

  – Is it better not to say anything? Or perhaps say something like, 'I'm sure you'll be back to your old self soon'?

- Your friend has bought some new clothes, but you think they look terrible.

  – Do you tell the truth and say that they look bad?

  – Or do you lie and say that they look good?

  – Are there any other options?

  – Which is most helpful to your friend in the long run?

You may wish to discuss the concept of a 'white lie' with the children at this point.

Give this final scenario:

- Your parents have cooked a special meal for your birthday, but you don't like it.

Ask the children to suggest responses, and discuss the consequences of each.

5 *Show slide 7.* Finish by explaining to the children that the truth can sometimes be hard to tell and to hear.

Sometimes we might tell a 'white lie' to protect someone else's feelings, but most of the time telling the truth is the best policy. The truth can be something difficult to say or something that someone doesn't want to hear, but in the end, being honest is the most helpful thing to do.

Emphasise, however, that it is really important that we always do tell the truth in a sensitive way.

Assembly 20
Trust

Overview

An assembly which highlights the importance of knowing who to trust, and of being trustworthy.

Key message

Trust is very important in a relationship.

Resources

- Blindfold or scarf
- PE mat
- A clip from *The Jungle Book* of the song 'Trust in Me', sung by Kaa the snake – the clip is widely available online.
- Slideshow 6
- A screen to display the slideshow

Set-up requirements

Set up the screen to display the slideshow and the clip.

Outline

1 Explain that today we are talking about the idea of trust and what it means. Ask the children for a definition of trust, and take a few suggestions.

The definition of trusting a person is to believe that they are honest and will not harm you on purpose. Having trust in an object involves believing it is reliable and will work as expected.

2 Show a clip from *The Jungle Book* of the song 'Trust in Me', sung by Kaa the snake – the clip is widely available online.

Ask the children for their thoughts about the clip. Should they trust Kaa?

3 Ask for a volunteer who feels that they can trust you. Invite the volunteer to the front of the assembly, ask them to stand on the PE mat and explain that you will blindfold them. When they are blindfolded, explain that you will catch them if they lean back and let themselves fall. Check they are OK with this and then ask them to do so if they are.

Emphasise that they needed to trust you to keep them safe: they had to show complete trust in you. Be clear that the children should not try this activity themselves without an adult, in any circumstances.

4 Work through the slideshow (*slides 2–6*), which shows different situations in which trust is needed. Ask the children to identify where and how trust is required in each situation.

- Nurse caring for a child: the child trusts that the nurse will care for them and help them as much as they can.

- Police officers: we trust police officers to be fair and uphold the law correctly.

- Parent with child: children trust their parents or guardians to look after them and care for them.

- A person with their guide dog: the person trusts their dog to guide them correctly and safely.

- A climber: the climber has to trust that their rope is secure, and also trust themselves and their own skill to keep them safe.

5 Finish by emphasising the following:

- The children and their parents should trust that school staff, as adults and experienced professionals, will look after them all, keep them safe, help them learn, support them, make sure they are happy, and ensure that everyone keeps to the school rules.

- The adults in the children's lives are also trusting them to do the right thing too: to be responsible, behave well, try hard and do their best.

- The children could also think about animals or pets that trust them to look after them, and the friends who they trust to help, encourage and support them.

Show slide 7.

We all need to know who we can trust but we also need to show everyone else that they can trust us. Explain that we can do this by listening, by asking questions, by making sure we keep promises, and by being honest and reliable.

Assembly 21
The Bigger Picture

Overview

This assembly encourages children not to rush into rash judgements or actions, but to look closely and to question what they see.

Resources

- Slideshow 7
- A screen to display the slideshow

Key message

It is important to take time to listen to all sides of a story, and not rush into making a judgement before knowing the facts.

Set-up requirements

Set up the screen to display the slideshow.

Outline

1 Explain to the children that this assembly is about fully understanding what we see.

2 Show the children the optical illusions on *slides 2 and 3*.

In the first, people see either an old woman looking left or a younger woman looking away.

In the second, people either see a goblet (the black area) or two people's faces shown side on (the white areas either side of the central black area).

Emphasise that different children will see different things; some won't see anything, and that is absolutely fine.

3 *Show slide 4*. Tell the children you are going to tell them one of the best-known folk tales from Wales, known as the legend of Bedd Gelert ('dd' is pronounced 'th'). Emphasise that it is a legend.

The Legend of Bedd Gelert

Hundreds of years ago there lived a Welsh prince called Llewelyn. He was a keen hunter and kept a large pack of the best hunting dogs in Wales. His favourite of all the dogs was a faithful hound called Gelert. Not only was he a skilled hunting dog, but he was also good-natured and friendly. He was much loved by Llewelyn and his family.

One day, Prince Llewelyn heard that a pack of wolves had been seen in the local area near his castle, and this worried him. Wolves had been known to attack his villagers in the past, so, after telling Gelert to guard his baby son, he and his men set off in search of the wolves. Llewellyn trusted the dog completely and knew that his son would be safe with Gelert to protect him.

Some time later, Gelert, alone in the castle with the baby, smelt a most unusual smell and heard a strange sound in the baby's bedroom. He wondered what this was, so he pushed open the large oak door to the baby's bedroom. To his horror, he was confronted with the sight of an enormous wolf with fierce yellow eyes, its teeth bared, its mouth drooling, looking hungrily at the baby sleeping peacefully in its cot.

Gelert growled angrily at the wolf, which howled and leapt onto the cot. But Gelert jumped to protect the baby, and the cot was knocked over. Thankfully the baby was unhurt and landed on his blankets, where he carried on sleeping behind the upturned cot.

Meanwhile, Gelert and the wolf fought viciously. Blood and fur flew all over the room, and screams of pain from both dog and wolf could be heard far away in the castle grounds.

After a long fight, Gelert sank his teeth into the wolf's throat. The wolf collapsed to the floor, dead. Gelert, drained of strength and exhausted, sank to the floor to lick his bleeding wounds.

Llewelyn returned to the castle where he saw a terrible sight. His baby son's cot was upside down, there was blood everywhere and the baby was nowhere to be seen. The faithful Gelert was delighted to see his master and crawled slowly towards Llewelyn, full of pride.

'Where is my son?' shouted Llewelyn. 'You have killed him and eaten him! My baby boy! You wicked dog!'

With an ear-piercing cry, he pulled out his sword and thrust it into Gelert's heart. Gelert howled in agony and sorrow. This woke the baby, who started to cry. Llewelyn looked behind the cot, where he saw his son, safe and well, right next to the body of an enormous grey wolf.

Llewelyn immediately realised his terrible mistake. He had assumed that Gelert had attacked his beloved child, when in fact the blood on Gelert belonged to the wolf, not his son. Gelert had in fact protected his son bravely from the wolf.

The prince's heart was filled with sadness and pain and he never smiled again. The legend goes that he buried his faithful dog at a place he named Beddgelert, which means 'the grave of Gelert'. The village is still there today, in North Wales.

4 Explain how 'seeing things clearly' sometimes involves taking your time, stepping back and thinking carefully. Explain that when people are angry or experiencing strong emotions, they often act without thinking and can regret it afterwards.

5 Explain that it is always very important to 'see' or 'use one's eyes' properly.

- Discuss how 'seeing', in the broadest sense, is one of the most important skills. It's important to be able to observe closely and carefully, to 'read' situations and people, and to see all sides of an argument.

- Explain how staff in schools need to be able to do this: to assess who is learning, to know who needs help or has something to say, and to sort out disputes between children.

Show slide 5.

We all need to listen to each other's point of view so that we understand things clearly.

Assembly 22
Standing on the Shoulders of Giants

· ·

Overview

An assembly that explores the value of humility by looking briefly at Isaac Newton's achievements and his acknowledgment of other people's hard work.

Key message

We should appreciate everybody's contribution, no matter how large or small. Even the most brilliant and talented people can be humble.

Resources

- An apple and a telescope, or pictures of these items
- Slideshow 8
- A screen to display the slideshow

Set-up requirements

Set up the screen to display the slideshow.

Outline

1 *Show slide 1.* Ask the children if they know what 'humility' means. Remind the children of the meaning: being modest and not being too proud, stubborn or arrogant to admit your mistakes or say sorry.

2 *Show slide 2.* Ask what the connection between a £2 coin and humility might be.

   There are unlikely to be any correct guesses, so draw attention to the wording on the edge of a £2 coin: 'standing on the shoulders of giants'.

3 Tell the children that these are the words of a very famous scientist. Can they guess who?

   Show slide 3 to give the children the clues of an apple and a telescope. Hold up the props if you have them.

   If no one guesses, explain that the person you are thinking of is Isaac Newton. *Show slide 4.*

   Explain that Newton was a very talented scientist and mathematician, born in 1643. Read the quote aloud: 'If I have seen further it is by standing on the shoulders of giants.' Ask the children what they think the phrase 'standing on the shoulders of giants' might mean.

4 Explain the following:

· Newton is regarded as a genius, but he was still ready to recognise the work that other people had already done, which he built on and developed.

· The quote shows that Newton had a humble view of himself. He didn't mean that he had literally stood on giants' shoulders! Newton actually meant that many scientists had done great work before him and all he did was to take their work even further. This illustrates his modesty and humility.

5 Talk about some of Newton's achievements and discoveries. *Show slide 5.*

· Seeing an apple fall to the ground helped him become the first person to understand and explain the idea of gravity.

· He built the first reflecting telescope. By using a mirror to reflect the image of the stars, it was possible to see far more than with the ordinary optical telescope.

· He also discovered how white light can be divided into colours, as we see in a rainbow.

6 *Show slide 6* and read the quote.

'I don't know what I may seem to the world, but as to myself, I seem to have been only like a boy playing on the sea-shore and diverting myself in now and then finding a smoother pebble or a prettier shell than ordinary, whilst the great ocean of truth lay all undiscovered before me.'

Explain why this quote illustrates Newton's humility and modesty even further: he knew his knowledge was limited and there was much more to be found out and learnt.

Remind the children that humility is also about letting your light shine without telling everyone or expecting a reward.

7 Finish by asking the children to think about their reasons for doing the things they do. *Show slide 7.*

· Do you sometimes do things because it benefits you alone, or because it makes you look good?

· Do you do things to impress others or because it's the right thing to do?

· When was the last time you did something because you knew it would help or benefit other people, rather than just yourself?

· How often do you do something quietly without boasting about it?

· Could you try and think of something you could do to help others today?

· Could you secretly do a kind deed for someone this week?

Assembly 23
Courage

Overview

This assembly explores how the children might feel when faced with dangerous situations, and demonstrates how people are able to show great strength and courage at difficult times.

Key message

We all need to be courageous at some point in our lives. It may not always be in a dramatic way, like Grace Darling's story, but we need to be aware that we will all face challenges that will need to be overcome.

Resources

- *The Hebrides* overture by Mendelssohn: www.youtube.com/watch?v=zcogD-hHEYs
- *Storm* – movement 4 of Benjamin Britten's *Sea Interludes*: www.youtube.com/watch?v=xQwmb8aE5uk
- Speakers
- A device to play the music
- Slideshow 9
- A screen to display the slideshow

Set-up requirements

Set up the screen to display the slideshow.

Set up the speakers to play the music clips.

Outline

1 *Show slide 2.* Play a short extract from *The Hebrides* overture by Mendelssohn as the children enter the assembly room. Explain that this music was inspired by Mendelssohn's visit to a sea cave in Scotland.

2 Show the pictures of stormy seas on *slide 3*.

Explain that today you will be talking about courage. Ask the children to reflect on how they would feel if they were faced with the conditions as shown in slide 3.

- Why they would need courage to be, for example, on board a ship in such severe conditions?

Play *Storm* – movement 4 of Benjamin Britten's *Sea Interludes* while they reflect on this for a few minutes.

3 Tell the children you're going to share a story about someone who demonstrated great courage in a storm at sea. This happened nearly two hundred years ago in 1838, when ships were made of wood and sailing was much more dangerous than nowadays.

Show the picture of Grace Darling on *slide 4*.

Grace Darling's story

Grace Darling was the daughter of a lighthouse keeper. Her father looked after a lighthouse on the Farne Islands, off the coast of Northumberland in north-east England. His job was to make sure the lighthouse shone its light all the time to warn ships of the rocks nearby.

One stormy night, Grace spotted a ship on the rocks and warned her father. They realised that the storm was so fierce even the lifeboat wouldn't be able to reach the ship, as it had to come from further away. So Grace and her father decided to go to the rescue themselves in their small boat.

When they reached the ship, Grace held the rowing boat in position on the stormy waters while her dad helped people off the rocks. In total, their actions saved the lives of nine people.

Grace Darling became famous for her courage – although she was modest and did not welcome the fame. Sadly, she died of tuberculosis, a lung disease, at the age of 26.

4 Finish by explaining that there are many different sorts of courage. Most of the courageous people in the world are not famous, but they are still inspirational because of the ways they have overcome difficulties or obstacles in their lives.

Show slide 5.

We all must show courage from time to time because all of us will face problems and difficulties at some point. We must never forget that when people we know are struggling, we should be ready to help them in any way we can.

Assembly 24
Standing up for Each Other

Overview

An assembly which encourages us to stand up to injustice, unfairness and bullying, and to speak out when we see others being treated badly.

Key message

We need to take responsibility for looking after each other and support others when they need it.

Resources

- Slideshow 10
- A screen to display the slideshow

Set-up requirements

Set up the screen to display the slideshow.

Outline

1 Show *slide 1* and explain the 'rules for today'.

- No bike riding
- Do not travel by car or by bus
- Shop between 3pm and 5pm only
- No going to the cinema or theatre

- No watching TV between 3pm and 8pm
- No swimming, football or tennis
- No sitting in garden after 6pm
- No walking in streets between 8am and 6pm

Ask the children the following questions.

- How would you feel about having to follow these rules?
- What about if these rules only applied to one group of people? For example, if only Year 5 had to follow the rules and everyone else could do as they wanted?
- How would you feel if you were in Year 5? How would you feel if you weren't in Year 5?

Explain that these were actual rules for Jewish people living in Nazi-occupied countries in World War II.

2 *Show slide 2.*

Explain that the situation for Jewish people became far worse over the years.

Under the Nazi regime, Jewish people were forced to wear badges like the one on the slideshow to show that they were Jews. Explain that *Jude* is German for Jew.

The Nazis eventually killed 6 million Jewish people purely because they were Jewish.

3 Show the map of Denmark and Greater Germany during World War II on *slide 3*.

· The Danes knew that, as a small country, they could never resist any German invasion, so they spent the years before the war promoting the idea of equality and anti-racism. As a result, when the Nazis did invade, most Danes refused to accept the Nazis' racist policies and attitudes.

· Denmark kept its own king and government. It cooperated with the Nazis but stood up for Danish Jews, who were fully integrated into Danish society.

· The Nazis put up with this because they needed Danish agricultural produce and didn't want lots of their soldiers tied up occupying Denmark. They wanted Denmark to be an example of how Europe could be run under Nazi domination and considered Danes to be similar to Germans.

· The Danes made it clear that harming the Jews would bring their cooperation to an end, which would force the Germans to fully occupy Denmark. The king told his prime minister, in private, that if the Nazis forced Danish Jews to wear a yellow star, he would wear one too.

· In October 1943, the Nazis issued an order to deport all Danish Jews to concentration camps. Instead, most people in Denmark helped to evacuate the Jews to neutral Sweden.

4 *Show slide 5* to summarise how effective the Danish help was.

· There were around 7,000 Jewish people in Denmark in 1943.

· Around 6,500 Danish Jews escaped the Nazis.

· 464 Jewish people were sent to Theresienstadt concentration camp.

· 102 Danish Jews died during the war.

5 Read this poem based on speeches by Martin Niemöller, who fought against the Nazis.

> First they came for the Communists
>
> And I did not speak out
>
> Because I was not a Communist.
>
> Then they came for the Socialists
>
> And I did not speak out
>
> Because I was not a Socialist.
>
> Then they came for the trade unionists
>
> And I did not speak out
>
> Because I was not a trade unionist.
>
> Then they came for the Jews
>
> And I did not speak out
>
> Because I was not a Jew.
>
> Then they came for me
>
> And there was no one left
>
> To speak out for me.

6 It is not always easy to know what to do when we see others being treated unfairly. Even though we know we should stand up to injustice, it can be hard to do.

We should all try to find the courage to speak out when we see others being treated badly and take our responsibility of looking after each other very seriously.

Assembly 25
William Blake

Overview

This assembly introduces the children to the life and work of William Blake.

Key message

It's important to listen to other people's views and appreciate their talents, as William Blake's life shows.

Resources

- Optional: a recording of the song *Jerusalem* by Hubert Parry
- Optional: speakers and a device to play the song
- Slideshow 11
- A screen to display the slideshow

Set-up requirements

Set up the screen to display the slideshow.

Optional: set up the speakers to play the song.

Outline

1 Show the engraving by William Blake on *slide 2*. Ask the children the following questions:

- How do you think the picture was produced? [Explain that it was engraved on steel plate and printed in black ink.]
- What is the picture about? Is the title a clue?
- Why is it called 'I Want!'?
- Has the picture got a message?

2 Discuss the concept of ambition.

- Is it always a good thing?
- Is there a difference between needing and wanting something?
- What ambitions have you got?

3 *Show slides 3 and 4*. Share some background information about William Blake and his life.

- William Blake was born in London on 28 November 1757.
- He never went to school but was educated at home by his mother.
- At 14, he became apprenticed to an engraver, who made images like the one shown earlier, and spent the next seven years learning how to be an engraver.

- Blake was married to a woman called Catherine Boucher.

- Blake engraved the words of his poems and surrounding designs on copper – a method he claimed he had received in a dream. Catherine helped to colour the engravings and bind the books. Most of Blake's work sold slowly during his lifetime, so he was poor for much of his life.

- In 1803, Blake was involved in a fight with a soldier. He was charged with assault but also treason – a very serious offence, because he was supposed to have insulted the king. He was found not guilty.

- Blake had strong opinions on organised religion, and this made him unpopular with some people.

- His artwork and poetry were also quite unusual and many people didn't appreciate or like them, which made Blake unhappy and depressed.

- In recent times, many people have enjoyed and been influenced by Blake's work, including the band U2 and Maurice Sendak, who wrote the well-known children's book *Where The Wild Things Are*.

4 Explain that Blake's poems are often popular with young people because many of them have very powerful images. *Show slide 5*. Read his poem 'The Fly'.

'The Fly'
William Blake

Little fly
Thy summer's play,
My thoughtless hand
Has brush'd away.

Am not I
A fly like thee?
Or art not thou
A man like me?

For I dance
And drink and sing;
Till some blind hand
Shall brush my wing.

If thought is life
And strength and breath;
And the want
Of thought is death;

Then am I
A happy fly,
If I live,
Or if I die.

5 Tell the children that Blake held many unorthodox views which went against popular opinion and which sometimes got him into trouble. For example, he criticised the monarchy and the church, which were more powerful in society in those days than they are now. He also believed passionately in freedom and equality, and was against slavery, which was widespread at the time.

Show slide 6. Blake celebrated creativity and the imagination. He even taught himself to write backwards to make printing his work easier. Even though some people called him mad, he was certain that being able to think for yourself and having the freedom to have your own opinions were really important.

Emphasise to the children the importance of tolerance towards other peoples' views, and appreciation of their talents, even if you don't always agree with them.

6 Optional: Finish by playing the song *Jerusalem*, the lyrics to which are arguably Blake's most famous work.

Assembly 26
Change and Transition

Overview

An assembly which reassures children that change is natural and normal, yet acknowledges that it can also be worrying at times.

Resources

- A personal object or photo which represents a change in your life
- Slideshow 12
- A screen to display the slideshow

Key message

Change can help us develop and lead to exciting new opportunities and experiences.

Set-up requirements

Set up the screen to display the slideshow.

Outline

1 Show *The Metamorphosis of Narcissus* by Salvador Dali on *slide 2*.

   Explain that in Greek mythology, Narcissus was a vain young man who loved himself so much that he couldn't tear himself away from his reflection in a pond, and so he eventually died. The gods then turned him into a yellow flower.

   Explain that the picture is called *The Metamorphosis of Narcissus* and ask the children if they know what metamorphosis means.

   Give the definition: a major change that makes someone or something very different.

2 Show the picture of a caterpillar on *slide 3*. Ask the children why the caterpillar is an example of metamorphosis.

3 Show the picture of a butterfly on *slide 4* and ask if the children if they can think of other examples of metamorphosis in nature.

4 Show the picture of a tadpole and frog on *slides 5 and 6*.

   Explain that change happens in nature all the time: it's completely natural. Changes happen to humans too: remind them of the differences between a baby, a teenager and an older person.

   Tell the children you realise that change can also be a bit scary, and that is normal too.

   Share a personal example of change in your life, such as starting a new job or moving somewhere new. Show the children your personal object or photo linked to this event.

5 *Share slide 7.* Explain that this painting by Ford Maddox Brown shows two people on a ship who are seeing England for the last time as they set off on a journey to begin a new life in Australia. The painting was inspired by the painter's friend, who did exactly that.

6 Explain that, although there's nothing wrong with change, it's good that some things stay the same. There is nothing wrong with hanging on to things that are special and remind us of what we were like in the past.

7 *Show slide 8.* Finish by explaining that change is normal. Sometimes it can be scary, but it helps us to grow and develop and that is a good thing. Ask the children to think of themselves as a caterpillar: they would never become a beautiful butterfly if they were afraid of change!

Assembly 27
Black History Month

Overview

An assembly which teaches about Black History Month, and why it is important to celebrate inspirational individuals, events and the history of black communities in the UK.

Key message

Celebrating everyone's culture and history is an important way of ensuring equality for all of us.

Resources

- Slideshow 13
- A screen to display the slideshow

Set-up requirements

Set up the screen to display the slideshow.

Outline

1 Show the picture of Rosa Parks upon her arrest in December 1955, on *slide 2*.

Ask if anyone has heard of Rosa Parks.

Show slide 2. Explain that in 1955 in the USA, the law stated that black people had to sit at the back of the bus and give up their seats to white people when the bus was full. They were many other laws aimed at separating people because of their race. Rosa Parks refused to do this and was arrested. She was found guilty of 'disorderly conduct' and fined. She also lost her job as a result. Her arrest sparked a 381-day-long boycott of the local bus system by many people. The supreme court eventually declared that the law was wrong. The protest started the civil rights movement, which was the general struggle for equal rights for African Americans in the US.

Stress that treating people badly or differently because of the colour of their skin is wrong.

2 Show the picture of Olaudah Equiano on *slide 3*. Ask the children when they think he might have lived.

Show slide 3. Give a brief biography of Olaudah Equiano.

- Olaudah Equiano was a freed slave who lived from 1745–97.

- He was a prominent member of the 'Sons of Africa', a group who campaigned for the abolition of slavery in London.

- In 1789, he published his autobiography, *The Interesting Narrative of the Life of Olaudah Equiano or Gustavus Vassa, the African*.

Stress that although black people have been important in this country for hundreds of years, they have often been overlooked and have been largely 'written out' of history.

This is why Black History Month was created. The UK has celebrated Black History Month every October since 1987, but it has been celebrated worldwide since 1926.

3   Show the picture of Mary Seacole on *slide 4*.

Ask if anyone has heard of Mary Seacole. Give a brief biography. *Show slide 4.*

· Mary Seacole was born Mary Jane Grant in Jamaica in 1805.

· She learned her nursing skills from her mother and became a pioneering nurse.

· As they were mixed race, Mary and her family had few civil rights: they could not vote, hold public office or enter certain professions.

· She travelled all around the Caribbean and Central America. On these trips she complemented her knowledge of local medicine with European medical ideas.

· In 1854, Seacole travelled to England. While she was there, the lack of medical care for soldiers fighting in the Crimean War became known. She asked the War Office if she could be an army nurse in the Crimean War, but she was refused.

· So, Mary Seacole funded her own trip to the Crimea, where she established a hospital for sick and convalescent officers. She also visited the battlefield to nurse the wounded, and became known as 'Mother Seacole'.

· After the war she returned to England, destitute and in ill health.

· In 1857, she published her memoirs, *Wonderful Adventures of Mrs Seacole in Many Lands*. A benefit festival was organised to raise money for her, attracting thousands of people. She died in 1881.

Explain that, just as the history of wars is written by the 'winners', many histories of the world have been written by and focused on white Europeans and North Americans. For example, many people argue Mary Seacole's nursing contribution was more or equally important as that of Florence Nightingale, who more people have heard of.

4   Show the picture of George Washington Carver on *slide 5*. George Washington Carver was another remarkable and influential black person in history who many people have not heard of. *Show slide 5.*

· He was born in America in 1864, the son of a slave.

· He and his mother and sister were kidnapped by bandits on horseback. George was later found but never saw his mother or sister again. He never knew who his father was.

· As a sickly child, he was not able to work in the fields, but helped in the kitchen and showed great skill at cooking and needlework.

· He was passionately interested in plants and flowers which he took apart and studied. He walked great distances to get soil samples and find the best soils for certain plants.

· He did lots of different jobs, such as cook, farm labourer and laundryman, while getting an education.

· After being rejected from one university because he was black, he managed to get a degree at another, Iowa State Agricultural College. When he passed his final exam at the age of 35, he was offered a teaching job at the university. Two years later he qualified as Dr Carver.

· George Washington Carver went to teach at the Tuskegee Institute, which was set up by the well-known educator, Booker T. Washington, to offer educational opportunities to African Americans. He remained in this job for the rest of his life and never asked for a pay rise. When he became known across the USA, he was offered large salaries but turned them all down because he wanted to stay helping his students.

- As a plant scientist, he taught farmers how they could grow more and better crops. He found hundreds of new uses for the peanut, from peanut butter to cough mixture, and developed hundreds of products from the sweet potato, including gum used on postage stamps. He gave away all his discoveries because he just wanted to help people. His discoveries had a big impact as farming in the south had been struggling.

- When he died, the following was written on his tombstone: 'He could have added fortune to fame, but caring for neither, he found happiness and honour in being helpful to the world.'

5 Show the Eight Virtues for Students by George Washington Carver on *slide 6*.

These values were created by George Washington Carver.

Ask the children to think carefully about each one as you read them aloud.

- Do they think these values are still applicable 150 years later?

- Should we all be living by George Washington Carver's virtues?

> 1 Be clean both inside and out.
>
> 2 Neither look up to the rich or down on the poor.
>
> 3 Lose, if need be, without squealing.
>
> 4 Win without bragging.
>
> 5 Always be considerate of women, children, and older people.
>
> 6 Be too brave to lie.
>
> 7 Be too generous to cheat.
>
> 8 Take your share of the world and let others take theirs.

Point out that number 5 is perhaps the only one which is outdated. At the time, women were seen as weaker than men, and therefore in need of looking after in the same way as children. Explain that we could update this, perhaps to 'Always be considerate of other people'.

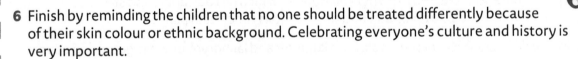

6 Finish by reminding the children that no one should be treated differently because of their skin colour or ethnic background. Celebrating everyone's culture and history is very important.

Show slide 7. Black History Month is an important way of highlighting the achievements of black people to help ensure equality for now and in the future.

Assemblies for All © Paul Stanley, 2021

Assembly 28
Bullying

Overview

This assembly defines bullying and suggests strategies to deal with it.

Key message

We need to be able to recognise bullying and have the courage to deal with it appropriately. It is important to recognise and celebrate the fact that we are all unique and different, but we should not use this as a reason for isolating and hurting people.

Resources

- Four A4 pieces of card with the following words written on them: 'deliberate / on purpose'; 'more than once'; 'causes hurt or harm'; and 'victim feels powerless'.
- Slideshow 14
- A screen to display the slideshow

See www.anti-bullyingalliance.org.uk for more information and tools.

Set-up requirements

Set up the screen to display the slideshow.

Outline

1 Ask the children to say what they think 'bullying' is. Steer their responses to show that bullying isn't always physical and doesn't always happen face to face. Try to get the children to talk about bullying online or via their phones.

2 Show the definition of bullying on *slide 2*. Explain it clearly to ensure everyone understands.

   The Anti-Bullying Alliance defines bullying as: 'the repetitive, intentional hurting of one person or group by another person or group, where the relationship involves an imbalance of power. It can happen face to face or online'.

3 Ask for four volunteers to come to the front to hold up the cards. Discuss each point in turn.

4 Show the six main types of bullying show on *slide 3* and expand on this.

   - Physical bullying: this includes any form of violence, such as pushing, hitting or kicking.

   - Verbal bullying: this includes insults, persistent teasing, spreading rumours or making threats.

   - Emotional bullying: this includes actions such as ignoring someone, hiding their possessions or embarrassing them.

   - Racial bullying: this includes racial insults and choosing to target someone because of their race.

   - Sexual bullying: this includes unwanted physical contact and inappropriate or abusive comments, particularly about people's appearance.

- Cyberbullying: this includes insults sent via text messages or on social media, comments on social media posts and setting up 'hate websites'.

5 Ask the children to look at the child next to them and think of at least one similarity and one difference between them. Focus on the idea that our differences make us unique – but that we also have much more in common than we have differences.

Tell the children that they should be confident and proud of the things that make them different and that they should respect and celebrate the differences they see in others.

6 Show and read aloud *slides 4 and 5*, which explain why people bully others and what you can do if you are being bullied.

Explain the different reasons why some people bully others:

- It gives them a feeling of power.

- They feel insecure, inadequate, humiliated, bored or frustrated.

- They have been abused or bullied themselves.

- They are under pressure to succeed at all costs.

- They don't feel that they fit in with other people.

- They are jealous of others.

- They become 'temporary bullies' after traumatic events.

- They are spoilt and expect everyone to do as they say.

Explain the different things you can do about bullying:

- Get help. Bullying makes you feel scared and unhappy – you need support.

- Tell someone. It might feel scary, but staying silent means the bully has won.

- Pretend to be confident, even if you are scared inside.

- Laugh at or ignore bullies' comments. Bullies want a reaction – don't give it to them.

- If a group is bothering you, say 'This isn't funny' or 'Go away!', then walk away. Practise doing this confidently in the mirror.

- Stay with a crowd – bullies often pick on people on their own.

- Do not stop if bullies confront you – just keep going.

- Ask witnesses to help you tell a teacher.

- Keep a diary of the events – when, where and what happened.

- Sign up for self-defence courses – not to fight, but to help your confidence.

Try 'fogging'. Imagine a 'fog' around you that swallows up insults so they can't get to you and affect you. 'Fogging' gives us a way to stop the things the bully says hurting us and also prevents us retaliating, responding inappropriately or making the situation worse. Remember that bullies want a particular reaction from you, so surprise them!

Ask for six volunteers to come to the front to practise this technique with you. Ask each child to separately shout "You're stupid!" at you. Give a different response each time:

- "That's kind, thank you!"
- "Is that a problem for you?"
- "I'm not really interested in your opinion."
- "If calling me stupid makes you feel better about yourself, I'm glad I can help."
- "Yes I might be. Never mind, eh?"
- "Well done, that's very observant of you."

Ask the children how they felt when you responded to them. Reiterate that these responses can often confuse the bully.

7 *Show slide 6.* Emphasise that it is very important for the children to seek support and to tell a trusted adult if they feel they are being bullied. Remind them that if bullies are making them upset, having support will make a difference.

8 *Show slide 7.* Remind the children that we all have the power to make or break someone's day by what we say or how we make them feel.

9 Finish by reminding the children that it is important to recognise and celebrate the fact that we are all unique and different. We should not use this as a way of isolating and hurting people. We are all the same underneath and have the same feelings.

We need to be able to recognise and understand bullying and have the courage to deal with it. We should always speak out against it and tell an adult if it is happening to us or someone we know.

Assembly 29
Art and Creativity

Overview

This assembly explains that people can show creativity in many ways: art, in its many different forms, is just one way.

Key message

There are many ways of being creative.

Resources

- Optional: a picture of one of your favourite pieces of art
- Slideshow 15
- A screen to display the slideshow

Set-up requirements

Set up the screen to display the slideshow.

Outline

1 Start the assembly by asking who thinks they are 'good at art'. Ask the children what exactly they think being 'good at art' means.

2 Explain that today's assembly will explore the work of some accomplished artists. You will be asking the children to think about art and creativity.

3 Share the definition of creativity on *slide 2*.

- Being inventive and thinking of original ideas
- Making an object or coming up with a plan, solution or concept

Discuss what art is. It's often defined as works, such as paintings or pieces of music, which express messages or ideas, often of beauty.

Share some ideas about what art is for. *Show slide 3.*

- For the artist to express themselves
- To get people thinking
- To make a point
- To help people express emotions and feelings (from anger to joy)
- To enjoy looking at
- For decoration
- To cheer people up
- To help people relax

Share the pictures of Andy Goldsworthy's art on *slide 4*. Discuss with the children whether they think it is art.

Show slide 5. Share some thoughts about why it might be art, as it is:

- Creative

- Technically skilful

- Imaginative

- Thought-provoking

- Has a message: it makes you appreciate nature and the environment

Discuss further ideas about what art is. *Show slide 6.*

- Is it the only way to be creative?

- Can you be an artist without being skilful? For example, without being amazing at painting or drawing? Or is it more important to have creative ideas?

- Have your opinions about art changed?

Reiterate that we can all be creative in many ways, and that art can include many more things than the children might think. Encourage them all to be creative as often as they can.

4 Optional: To finish, you may like to share your piece of art with the children and explain why you find it beautiful or interesting.

Assembly 30
Hopeless People

Overview

An assembly which looks at the lives of several well-known people who were not immediately successful, to show that we should all keep persevering.

Key message

Sometimes we need to work hard and persevere to be successful.

Resources

- A recording of the song *In The Ghetto* by Elvis Presley
- Speakers
- A device to play the song
- Slideshow 16
- A screen to display the slideshow

Set-up requirements

Set up the screen to display the slideshow.

Set up the speakers to play the song.

Outline

1 Play the song *In The Ghetto* by Elvis Presley as the children enter.

2 Explain that this assembly is all about people who are or were very talented and successful but to start off with, they were rejected or ignored. They persevered and were ultimately successful. The children may not have heard of some of them, but their stories are useful lessons.

3 Show the picture of Elvis Presley on *slide 2*.

Explain that Elvis Aaron Presley was an American singer (and actor). He is often known as the 'King of Rock and Roll' due the impact he had on music. He lived from 1935–77.

Elvis Presley went on to sell more than one billion records globally, but after his very first performance his manager said, 'You ain't goin' nowhere, son. You ought to go back to drivin' a truck.' Despite this, he carried on and became one of the most significant musicians in the 20th century.

4 *Show slide 3* – Entertainment.

Oprah Winfrey

Oprah's first boss told her she was too emotional and not right for television. But by 2011, Oprah was the best-paid woman in the entertainment industry and was the first black female billionaire.

Sidney Poitier

After his first audition, Poitier was told by the casting director, 'Why don't you stop wasting people's time and go out and become a dishwasher or something?' Luckily he didn't do this, and in 1964 he became the first black actor to win an Oscar for best actor. He is still admired today.

5 *Show slide 4* – Scientists and Engineers.

Henry Ford

Henry Ford was an inventor, engineer and entrepreneur who lived from 1863–1947. He founded Ford Motor Company, the car manufacturer which is still successful today. He spent all the money from his first group of investors without producing a passenger car, so the investors stopped giving him money. He then founded a new company, Ford, which went on to be extremely successful.

Henry Ford is known for having said, 'Failure is simply the opportunity to begin again, this time more intelligently.'

Albert Einstein

Albert Einstein (1879–1955) was a German-born theoretical physicist who developed the theory of relativity, among other discoveries.

Albert Einstein had a difficult time at school: one teacher told him he would never achieve anything, and he struggled to follow the strict rules; he ran away from one school. He went on to revolutionise science's understanding of the world and win the Nobel Prize.

6 *Show slide 5* – Authors.

Stephen King

Before becoming an iconic thriller, Stephen King's first book, *Carrie*, was rejected by 30 publishers. He had thrown an early version of this book in the bin, but his wife retrieved it and urged him to finish it. King has since published more than 50 books, all worldwide bestsellers.

J. K. Rowling

Her manuscript of *Harry Potter and the Philosopher's Stone* was rejected by 12 different publishers. 'By every usual standard, I was the biggest failure I knew,' said J.K. Rowling, who went from living on benefits to becoming the world's first billionaire author. She has given away much of her earnings to charity but remains one of the wealthiest people in the world.

7 *Show slide 6.* Finish by reminding the children that all the people you have just been discussing did not achieve success immediately. They did not give up after failing, but worked hard and persevered before eventually achieving their goals. Reiterate that we should all do the same: we should keep trying, even if things don't always work out as we would like them to.

Assembly 31
Reading and Dr Seuss

Overview

An assembly which promotes enjoyment of reading and encourages children to have fun, self-belief, and to be themselves.

Key message

Reading can be great fun!

Resources

- Optional: a selection of Dr Seuss books
- Slideshow 17
- A screen to display the slideshow

Set-up requirements

Set up the screen to display the slideshow.

Outline

1 Explain that today you are looking at the work of a very famous author and illustrator, known as Dr Seuss. *Show slide 2.*

He was born and lived in the USA but also went to university in the UK and France. His birth name was Theodor Seuss Geisel, but he adopted the name Dr Seuss when publishing books. He started out as an illustrator, including illustrating some things for adverts.

Mention that Dr Seuss wrote *The Cat in the Hat* and *How the Grinch Stole Christmas!*, which the children may have heard of.

2 *Show slide 3.* Read the quote aloud.

'The more that you read, the more things you will know. The more that you learn, the more places you'll go.' *I Can Read with My Eyes Shut!* by Dr Seuss

3 *Show slide 4.* Dr Seuss's books are famous for their rhymes. They usually also include an important message. For example, *Green Eggs and Ham* is about trying new things and not judging them by their appearance. *The Lorax* was written nearly 50 years ago, and is about caring for the environment.

4 Go through slides 5–9 one by one and ask the children to guess the end of each line before reading it.

> Don't give up
> I believe in you all
> A person's a person
> No matter...
> [Answer]...how small!
>
> *Fox in Socks* by Dr Seuss

And will you succeed?
Yes! You will, indeed!
(98 and 3/4 percent...
[Answer]...guaranteed.)

Oh, The Places You'll Go! by Dr Seuss

You have brains in your head
You have feet in your shoes
You can steer yourself
In any direction...
[Answer]...you choose.

Oh, The Places You'll Go! by Dr Seuss

You'll never be bored
When you try something new
There's really no limit...
[Answer]...to what you can do.

Dr Seuss

Today you are you
That is truer than true
There's no one alive
Who's more you-er than...
[Answer]...you!

Oh, The Places You'll Go! by Dr Seuss

5 *Show slide 10.* Finish by reminding the children that it is important to have fun when they are reading. Point out that there are books for every interest and reading level.

Assembly 32
How are we viewed by others?

Overview

This assembly looks at the legacy of Alfred Nobel, and discusses the impact we all have on the world, whether negative or positive.

Resources

- Slideshow 18
- A screen to display the slideshow

Key message

It is up to us to choose how we are viewed by other people. It is never too late to change someone's opinion of us.

Set-up requirements

Set up the screen to display the slideshow.

Outline

1 Start by showing *slide 1* as the children enter.

   Ask if anyone has heard of Alfred Nobel. Do they know why he is famous?

2 *Show slide 2.* Explain that Alfred Nobel was born in Stockholm, Sweden in 1833. He was a chemist, engineer, inventor and businessman.

   Also explain that, among other things, Alfred Nobel invented dynamite. Dynamite is an explosive substance. It was used to blow up large sections of earth, for example, to make tunnels or expand mines, but also used in weapons. By the time of his death, Nobel's business empire included more than 90 factories which made explosives and ammunition for weapons.

3 *Show slide 3.* In 1888, a strange incident happened. It was reported in newspapers that Alfred Nobel had died but this was a mistake: it was actually his older brother who had died.

   Because of his involvement with weapons, some of the descriptions of his life were critical: one newspaper report described him as a 'merchant of death'.

4 *Show slide 4.* When Alfred Nobel actually died in 1896, he left most of his huge fortune to fund five prizes to celebrate and encourage achievements in the fields of Chemistry, Physics, Medical Sciences, Literature and Peace which benefited humanity. It's thought that the experience of seeing the critical newspaper reports about his life prompted him to reflect and decide to use his fortune from destructive things to fund something positive and beneficial.

5 *Show slides 5 and 6* and briefly outline the history of each Nobel Prize recipient.

   European Union, 2012

   - The European Union began as a project in the 1950s to encourage European countries to work and trade together in the aftermath of the divisions of World War II.

- The prize was given because 'for over six decades [it] contributed to the advancement of peace and reconciliation, democracy and human rights in Europe'.

Malala Yousafzai, 2014

- Malala Yousafzai grew up in Pakistan and fought for education for girls, which was banned or discouraged. She was shot because of this, but survived.

- She has continued to work for education for all.

- Her prize was given 'for her struggle against the suppression of children and young people and for the right of all children to education'.

Barack Obama, 2009

- Barack Obama was President of the United States for eight years and the first black person to become president.

- His prize was given 'for his extraordinary efforts to strengthen international diplomacy and cooperation between peoples'.

Nelson Mandela and F. W. de Klerk, 1993

- These two men lived in South Africa, which for a long time had a system called apartheid, under which black people and white people were separated and black people were treated very badly. They were responsible for ending the system.

- They were given the prize for ensuring the peaceful ending of the 'apartheid regime, and for laying the foundations for a new democratic South Africa'.

6 Explain that Alfred Nobel was lucky to have the opportunity to think about his impact on the world. He chose to use this in a positive way. Point out that we can all try to have a positive impact on the world around us, even if it is not in as significant a way as Alfred Nobel's prizes.

7 *Show slide 7*. Finish by asking the children to think about the following questions:

- What do you think people's opinion is of you?

- Is there anything you could do to make people feel even more positive about you?

Assembly 33
Homophobia

Overview

An assembly which reinforces that difference and diversity should be respected.

Resources

- Slideshow 19
- A screen to display the slideshow

Key message

It is important to celebrate our differences. People should not be treated differently because of their sexuality.

Set-up requirements

Set up the screen to display the slideshow.

Outline

1 *Show slide 2*. Oscar Wilde lived from October 1854 to November 1900. His famous books include *The Importance of Being Earnest* and *The Picture of Dorian Gray*. Read out some quotes from him and discuss them with the children.

- 'Always forgive your enemies – nothing annoys them so much.'

- 'Experience is simply the name we give our mistakes.'

- 'The only thing worse than being talked about is not being talked about.'

Ask: What do you think about them? Do you agree with him?

2 *Show slide 3*. Oscar Wilde was imprisoned for two years with hard labour because he was homosexual, which was illegal at the time. The court case left him bankrupt and prison affected his health. He died aged 46. Oscar Wilde was a talented man whose life was ruined and cut short only because he was homosexual.

3 *Show slide 4*. Alan Turing was a brilliant mathematician, code breaker and computer scientist. He played a significant role in the development of the modern computer. He led the team responsible for breaking the German secret code ('Enigma') in WWII, shortening the war by an estimated two years and saving thousands, possibly millions of lives.

Show slide 5. Alan Turing was charged for being homosexual. He was given female hormones as an alternative to prison. He killed himself, aged 41, by eating an apple poisoned with cyanide.

4 *Show slide 6*. Justin Fashanu played in England's top football division for the teams Norwich and Nottingham Forest. He became well-known when he scored a wonder goal against a then dominant Liverpool side. He was the first black football player in the UK to be transferred for £1 million pounds.

Show slide 7. Justin Fashanu received lots of abuse when he announced he was homosexual. He killed himself aged 37. No other British male professional footballer has since stated they are homosexual while still a player. (The situation is very different in women's football, where several professional players are openly homosexual or bisexual.)

5 *Show slide 8*. Explain the situation today in the UK. Homosexuality and same-sex marriage are now legal. In 2013, Alan Turing was granted a royal pardon. A new law, nicknamed 'Turing's Law', has led to 65,000 other men being pardoned, as their convictions were unfair, unjust and discriminatory. However, people who are homosexual are still sometimes treated badly and with prejudice.

Show slide 9. Across the world, homosexuality is still illegal in some countries. In a few countries, the death penalty is still in place for this; others have harsh punishments.

6 *Show slide 10*. Explain the meaning of the word 'gay' – the same as 'homosexual'. Emphasise that it does not mean 'rubbish' or 'stupid', and it should not be used as an insult.

· It is disrespectful.

· In most cases, it will not be accurate.

· It is not acceptable.

· It is homophobic and against the law.

· It will not be tolerated in any school, just as racism and other bullying is not tolerated.

7 *Show slide 11*. Explain that it would be a boring world if everyone were exactly the same. We should respect everyone, including anyone who may be different to us. We certainly shouldn't use anyone's differences as a way to insult them. Finish by emphasising that in every school there will be some people who are heterosexual and some who are homosexual. Reinforce the importance of recognising and respecting difference and diversity.

Assembly 34
Thomas Edison and Perseverance

Overview

This assembly looks at the life, inventions and personality of Thomas Edison to explore the topic of perseverance.

Resources

- Slideshow 20
- A screen to display the slideshow

Key message

Success is rarely achieved without hard work and without initial failure. We need to remember not to give up, not to fear failure, and to learn from our mistakes.

Set-up requirements

Set up the screen to display the slideshow.

Outline

1   Start the assembly by asking pupils if they have heard of Thomas Edison. What do they know about him, if anything? Take some of their answers.

2   *Show slides 2 and 3* and discuss Edison's life and work.

He was born in 1847 in Ohio, USA; the seventh and last child of Samuel and Nancy Edison. When he was seven his family moved to Michigan,USA and he lived there until the age of 16. He had very little formal education as a child, attending school only for a few months. He was taught reading, writing and arithmetic by his mother. He was always a very curious child and taught himself much by reading on his own. This belief in self-improvement remained throughout his life.

Thomas Edison invented the phonograph (also known as the gramophone). This was the most common way of playing recorded music from the 1870s to the 1980s.

His other famous inventions were the lightbulb and the projector.

- Can you imagine life without lightbulbs?

Thomas Edison was partially deaf. Some of his first inventions were devices to help him with tasks which involved being able to hear well.

3   *Show slides 4–6* in turn and discuss each quote. These quotes by Edison illustrate his character. Ask the children to list the qualities of Edison's personality which probably contributed to his successes.

Assemblies for All © Paul Stanley, 2021

- 'Genius is one per cent inspiration and ninety-nine per cent perspiration. Accordingly, a genius is often merely a talented person who has done all of his or her homework.'

- 'The three great essentials to achieving anything worthwhile are: first, hard work, second, stick-to-it-iveness, and third, common sense.'

- 'I readily absorb ideas from every source, frequently starting where the last person left off.'

- 'To have a great idea, have a lot of them.'

- 'Someday, man will harness the rise and fall of the tides, imprison the power of the sun, and release atomic power.'

- 'Opportunity is missed by most people because it comes dressed in overalls and looks like work.'

- 'Just because something doesn't do what you planned it to do in the first place doesn't mean it's useless.'

- 'I am not discouraged, because every wrong attempt discarded is another step forward.'

- 'I never failed once. It just happened to be a 2000-step process.'

- 'I'm proud of the fact that I never invented weapons to kill.'

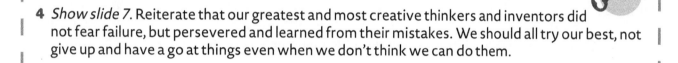

4 *Show slide 7*. Reiterate that our greatest and most creative thinkers and inventors did not fear failure, but persevered and learned from their mistakes. We should all try our best, not give up and have a go at things even when we don't think we can do them.

Assembly 35
Remembrance

Overview

This assembly looks at how we commemorate those who die in wars.

Resources

- Slideshow 21
- A screen to display the slideshow

Key message

It is important to remember all those who die in wars.

Set-up requirements

Set up the screen to display the slideshow.

Outline

1 *Show slide 1* and ask if the children know why 11 November is a significant date.

2 *Show slide 2.* Explain that 11 November is the anniversary of the end of World War I, which lasted from 1914 to 1918. It is known as Remembrance Day or Armistice Day in many countries around the world. Initially, the day was to commemorate those who died in World War I, in particular members of the armed forces. After World War II, the day has honoured all those who died in both world wars and all wars since. More than 7,000 service people have been killed in wars since World War II.

3 *Show slide 3* and ask the children to think about the families who have lost loved ones in war and conflicts over the years. Explain that we remember the service people who died fighting in wars through services and two minutes' silence.

Show slide 4. Read an extract from the poem 'For the Fallen' by Laurence Binyon. Explain that he volunteered with the French hospital services during World War I and his words are often used to commemorate those who died.

Extract from *For the Fallen*
by Laurence Binyon

They shall not grow old, as we that are left grow old;
Age shall not weary them, nor the years condemn.
At the going down of the sun and in the morning
We will remember them.

This may be a good time to ask the children to sit quietly for a minute's silence.

4 *Use slides 5 and 6* to explain the significance of poppies.

Poppy seeds grow well in soil which has been dug up or disturbed, so they were one of the first signs of life to grow on the battlefields after World War I was over. That is why they were chosen as a symbol of remembrance.

John McCrae, who fought in World War I, wrote a poem about poppies, which is often read during remembrance ceremonies.

Extract from *In Flanders Fields*
by John McCrae

In Flanders fields the poppies blow
Between the crosses, row on row,
That mark our place; and in the sky
The larks, still bravely singing, fly
Scarce heard amid the guns below.

We are the Dead. Short days ago
We lived, felt dawn, saw sunset glow,
Loved and were loved, and now we lie
In Flanders fields.

---

5 *Show slides 7, 8 and 9* and ask the children what they notice about these figures.

Estimated total of those killed in World War I: 21.5 million, of which 8.5 million were military deaths and 13 million were civilian deaths – people who weren't actively fighting.

Estimated total of those killed in World War II: 35.8 million, of which 19.7 million were military deaths and 17.4 million were civilian deaths. Note that this total is at the lower end of the possible number of deaths – the war was so vicious that it is impossible to know for certain how many people died as a result of it.

The ratio of civilian to military deaths in recent wars is difficult to calculate for certain, but what is definite is that over the past two hundred years, wars have gone from mainly involving only those actively fighting in them to affecting civilians more and more.

6 *Show slide 10* and ask if the children have seen white poppies before. Explain that for over 80 years, some people have preferred to wear white poppies, sometimes as well as a red poppy. The white poppies represent remembrance for all victims of war alongside a commitment to peace.

7 *Show slide 11.* Emphasise the human loss suffered during conflict and war and ask the children:

· Should we do more to prevent violence, conflict and war?

8 Finish with the quote from Gandhi on slide 11: 'I object to violence because when it appears to do good, the good is only temporary; the evil it does is permanent'. Briefly explain that Gandhi fought for India to be liberated from British control using peaceful means.

Reiterate the importance of working together to promote peace throughout the world.

Assembly 36
Female Scientists

Overview

This assembly celebrates the achievements of women in science, technology, engineering and maths (STEM).

Key message

We need to understand the significant contribution made by women in various areas of science.

Resources

- Slideshow 22
- A screen to display the slideshow

Set-up requirements

Set up the screen to display the slideshow.

Outline

1 *Show slide 2* and ask the children the question whether they can name any famous scientists. They might mention scientists such as Isaac Newton, Albert Einstein, Stephen Hawking, Brian Cox, or Charles Darwin.

   Do the children suggest any women, such as Marie Curie or Mary Anning? Point this out if they have not mentioned any women, or mentioned fewer women than men, and discuss the reasons for this with them.

2 Explain that you are going to introduce them to some female scientists.

   Show slide 3. Explain that Marie Curie is the only person to have won Nobel prizes for both Physics and Chemistry. Thanks to her work, cancer can be treated using radiation. Sadly, she died from exposure to radiation in the course of her scientific research.

3 *Show slide 4.* Hypatia lived in Alexandria, Egypt, around 1,600 years ago. She was one of the best mathematicians and astronomers in the world at the time she lived, and she also gave lectures on philosophy which attracted large audiences. Sadly, she was killed by an extremist mob of Christians who disagreed with her philosophy.

4 *Show slide 5.* Explain that Ada Lovelace was a brilliant mathematician who first saw the enormous potential of computers nearly 200 years ago. She studied with Mary Somerville, who was herself an amazing scientist.

5 *Show slides 6 and 7* and briefly list each scientist's achievements.

- Maggie Aderin-Pocock (b. 1968) – a space scientist, mechanical engineer and science communicator. She co-presents the BBC's astronomy programme *The Sky at Night*.

- Rosalind Franklin (1920–58) – a scientist who produced X-rays of DNA, a discovery which paved the way for the discovery of the structure of DNA. DNA makes up our genes, which determine how we look and how our bodies function.

- Wang Zhenyi (1778–97) – an astronomer, mathematician and poet. She researched the stars, planets and eclipses, wrote simplified maths texts to help beginners and wrote poems.

- Yoky Matsuoka (b. 1972) – chief technical officer at Google Nest, which makes a range of smart devices such as smart screens and speakers. She was previously an assistant professor at several universities and worked to develop better prosthetic limbs.

- Caroline Herschel (1750–48) – discovered eight comets, among other discoveries, and received a gold medal from the Royal Astronomical Society for her work.

- Jane Goodall (b. 1934) – a primatologist (someone who studies apes and monkeys) whose research on chimpanzees was ground-breaking and included the discovery that chimpanzees can use tools.

- Lise Meitner (1878–1968) – helped discover the process of nuclear fission, which is used to produce energy in nuclear power stations – as well as in atom bombs.

6 *Show slide 8*. Finish by explaining that women are still underrepresented in the fields of science and technology in the UK. Historically, women were not encouraged to study in these fields and we still see the results of this today. We need brilliant scientists to solve the world's problems, regardless of gender.

Index